THE LITERATURE OF JAZZ

a critical guide

by

DONALD KENNINGTON

American Library Association
Chicago 1971

Originally published in Great Britain in 1970 by
The Library Association (SBN 85365 074 8)

This edition published in 1971 by American Library
Association, Chicago, Illinois

International Standard Book Number 0-8389-0102-6 (clothbound);
0-8389-0105-0 (paperbound)

Library of Congress Catalog Card Number 74-151831

Printed in the United States of America

67796

To Pat

'. . . There were a raft of books published about jazz history, a lot of them bad, some of them very good as to facts and dates and names; a few were readable, the rest mostly for the fanatics and so packed with names, dates and written either in professors' English or reporters' prose that you had to love the stuff a lot to wade through it. But it all helped, it all made the subject serious because people are impressed by the printed word about anything.'

Stephen Longstreet *The real jazz, old and new*

CONTENTS

INTRODUCTION

The need for a guide to the rapidly growing literature of jazz music has been apparent for some time. In the forty or so years since the first book on the subject was written, some bibliographical work has been done, notably by Alan Merriam and Robert Reisner in America, but, to the best of my knowledge, there has never been an attempt at a critical appraisal.

Up to the beginning of the Second World War only a handful of books had appeared which made a serious attempt to analyse what jazz really was and from whence it came. Since that time the literature has proliferated, particularly in the late 1950's and early 1960's. The market for books on jazz may have been temporarily satiated but on the whole more discerning works are now appearing. Francis Newton discovered in 1959 that the serious listener to jazz in Britain belongs mainly to the grammar school-educated technocrat social group and probably to the 'reading' thirty per cent of this country. Public libraries therefore have a steady demand for books on all aspects of the subject but no British library has made any real effort to collect all the literature. Apart from the library of the Institute of Jazz Studies at Rutgers University, New Brunswick, the collections of the Library of Congress, Washington, and of some private collectors, it is doubtful whether a really comprehensive collection of the literature of jazz exists. As time passes the earlier works will disappear and the student will be unable to refer to necessary sources. My aim in producing this guide is to indicate to the beginner in jazz which are the significant works and to refresh the memory of the expert as to the books he has probably read in the past. I also hope to be able to indicate to the librarian both the books and journals he needs to stock in order to achieve a balanced collection and the sources he might try when locating information on the subject.

As the title of the work indicates, it is selective and some ephemeral (mainly pamphlet) literature has been omitted. It is felt, however, that all significant books published in the English language up to the end of 1969 have been listed. In each case all editions known to the author are given, except where Canadian and American editions have been published simultaneously. Coverage of foreign language material is restricted to the works of major critics such as Hodeir, Lange, Panassie and Goffin and to the bibliographical and reference sources which will guide the student to other items which cannot be included. A few selected items from the periodical literature are also quoted in the bibliographies which are appended to each chapter.

The arrangement attempts to be logical, with the general background material on African music, the American Negro and other primary ingredients of jazz, such as the blues and ragtime, coming in the first chapter together with literature on the sociological aspects. Historical writings on jazz generally and in the form of bibliographical works are covered in the next two chapters; there is considerable overlap between this material and that which is included in Chapter 4 on analysis and criticism. The reference sources covered in Chapter 5 proceed from coverage in the general encyclopedias, through the specialised works which include discographies and bibliographies. Chapter 6 deals with the periodical literature and Chapter 7 discusses jazz and the literary arts, particularly jazz fiction. The final chapter covers some of the main organisations in the field. There is a comprehensive index to book titles and a general index which includes authors and names of persons referred to in the text as well as to subject concepts. An appendix on 'Jazz on film' completes the guide.

Each chapter (except Chapter 3) is completed by a bibliography in alphabetical order of author in which all authors (with initials), titles and sub-titles, edition, place of publication, name of publisher and date are included. All

English language editions are given wherever possible. Citations from the journal literature are also included in some cases and these include title of journal in full, part number and pages. In many cases brief explanatory annotations are also included. In Chapter 3 references are arranged under the name of the biographee primarily and then alphabetically by author. For example:

Duke Ellington
GAMMOND, P. *ed. Duke Ellington.* London, Phoenix House, 1958.
LAMBERT, G. E. *Duke Ellington.* London, Cassell, 1959.

In Chapter 6 periodicals are listed by title and each citation includes full title, country of origin, dates (where known) and language where not English. Brief annotations are included in a few cases.

Chapter 9 includes a short list of jazz organisations. All items in the bibliographies are indexed. Each entry in the appendix includes film title, country of origin, date and a brief note of jazz musicians featured. The items asterisked are those with jazz scores.

The author has been interested in this field since 1946 but the actual preparation of the text has been done over the past four years. In this time help has been received from many individuals and corporate bodies in the United Kingdom and overseas. The staff of the Lindsey and Holland, Leicestershire County, and Lambeth Public Libraries were extremely helpful in obtaining literature and I have had substantial aid from the British Institute of Jazz Studies, particularly through Norman Lambert and Graham Langley. The Institute of Jazz Studies in the United States gave me much useful information, as did Joseph Balcerak (Poland), Paavo Einio (Finland), Arie Elings (Netherlands), Harry Nicolaussen (Sweden), Dieter Zimmerle (Germany), Clarence H. Hogue and Len Kunstadt (U.S.A.) and Brian Peerless, Doug Dobell, Frank Dixon, Peter Tanner, Bernard Holland, Les Page, Steve Lane and Simon Napier. Mary Kay Burns, Head of the Louisiana Division of the New Orleans Public Library, sent me extremely useful information on that Library's collections as well as some details of the

New Orleans Jazz Museum. A major part of the disco-graphy section in Chapter 5 is based on Paul B. Sheatsley's excellent 'state-of-the-art' article published in *Record Research* (No. 58. February 1964, pp. 3–6) and a special acknowledgment is made to this writer. John Marshall, David Dundas and Norman Day read and criticised the final draft of the work and Jack Haselgrove, my colleague in preparing previous bibliographical work on jazz, also contributed to my knowledge. James Tudor double checked many of the references and Mrs. Christine Akinkugbe typed and re-typed the manuscript many times without complaint. Both are thanked sincerely. Finally, the Guide would have been impossible to complete without the active guidance and encouragement of Derek Langridge. His influence on the final result is considerable but all errors and omissions are the full responsibility of the author alone.

Tunbridge Wells, 1970

LIST OF ABBREVIATIONS

Ed.	Edition *or* editor
M.A.	Master of Arts
N.Y.	New York
n.d.	no date
Ph.D.	Doctor of Philosophy
pseud.	pseudonym
U.K.	United Kingdom
U.S.A.	United States of America

CHAPTER 1

THE GENERAL BACKGROUND

Jazz was born at the end of the nineteenth century, although the musical forms which fused to bring it into being had already by then existed for many years. These musical forms include the chants and work songs of West Africa, the hymn tunes of eighteenth-century Britain (from which the spiritual ultimately developed), the popular dance and operatic music of France and the 'tinge' acquired from Spanish folk music. The Southern States, and particularly the port of New Orleans, were racial melting pots where these musical cultures coalesced over the years.

The African ingredient was mainly the rhythmic drive, emanating from Negro slaves, with the European influences coming from the settling immigrants. France and Spain dominated the area up to the Louisiana Purchase in 1803 and much of their musical heritage and culture remained after that time, particularly in the 'free-born' Creoles. Other Spanish influences came in from the nearby Caribbean islands like Cuba, which were at that time part of the Spanish Empire.

After the Civil War ended, the Negro looked for new ways to provide outlets for his natural exuberance. His musical instincts led him to make primitive home-made instruments, and these, together with trumpets, trombones and so on acquired from the disbanding Confederate Army, were used to produce a primitive home-made music. These early players of jazz were musically illiterate and their technique was acquired by trial and error with peculiar fingerings producing peculiar noises and effects. These effects were cultivated and are the forerunners of the many varied tone colours we have in jazz today. This folk music approach is, in some ways, similar to the early stirrings of European music, except that the latter had several centuries start. Music in this context was passed on from one performer to another and, because of illiteracy, nothing was documented. So it is that, in spite of the comparatively recent origins of jazz, much of its pre-history and indeed early history is shrouded in legend. The occasional white sociologist or musicologist showed some interest in the music of the Negroes, but few really understood it, since it grew out of the appalling living conditions endured by a race in bondage. This description is still apt for the post-Civil War period, since the actual conditions endured by many black Americans improved so very little. Contemporary developments such as the Civil Rights and Black Power movements provide evidence that American Negroes feel themselves still oppressed even today.''

The documentation of the gestation period of this explosive art form is thus negligible. The early periodical articles of the 'twenties were meagre, ill-informed and usually anti-jazz in outlook. European writers were the first to see some of the hidden realities. No doubt they were able to view with appropriate detachment, but this had its dangers since they came to wrong conclusions and put into print many erroneous statements.

The greatest single influence on the dissemination of knowledge about jazz was the invention of the disc-shaped gramophone record followed by the rapid development of radio in the 'twenties. Gramophone records made possible the preservation of fragments of jazz from 1916 onwards and their world-wide circulation created interest beyond the restricted areas of the United States where jazz first appeared.

It has proved difficult to decide what limitations to apply to the scope of this chapter. It could be said that the whole history of the Negro people in the United States is relevant since jazz and its major ingredients are closely bound up with their social and political experience.

The importation of African slaves has ultimately provided the United States with many major problems, but it has undoubtedly also produced for America its most genuine and original art form which has subsequently been exported to the whole world. Americans were, on the whole, very slow to recognise its importance and qualities, probably because of a national guilt-complex towards their black fellow-citizens. Perhaps the most important single book on the general subject of the American Negro is E. Franklin Frazier's *Negro in the United States* which was revised in 1957 and is a compendium of information on this subject. It is weak on jazz and popular music but it is an important basic work and includes a very full bibliography. Another work worthy of some study is *The American Negro reference book* (1966) which was edited by John P. Davis. It brings together in its 969 pages a reliable summary of current information on the main aspects of Negro life in America. It is all of interest as general background material and there are three particularly useful chapters to the jazz student. These are Chapter 20 on 'Negro music in American life' by Zelma George, Chapter 21 on 'Blues, jazz and the Negro' by Le Roi Jones and Chapter 24 on 'The Negro and American entertainment' by Langston Hughes.

The subject of African music is large in itself but, since some understanding of its rhythmic qualities are essential to any student of jazz, a work of interest is A. M. Jones *Studies in African music*. This deals primarily with the music of West Africa—the area from which most of the slaves originated. A more general *Folk and traditional music of western continents* by Dr. B. Nettl has chapters on 'African music south of the Sahara' and 'Negro folk music in the New World'. This is a scholarly work and the relevant chapters provide brief background information together with bibliographical and discographical sources.

The American slave trade is vividly described in *Black cargoes* by Mannix and Cowley, and other works on this infamous episode are *Slavery in America* by B. Hollander and *Slavery* by S. M. Elkins, all of which have been published in the past few years. Probably better than any book on this topic is Kenneth Stampp's *The peculiar institution* (1956), which is both a well documented and readable account of slavery in the Southern States.

American folk music is very well documented and there is space here to quote only a few of the more important titles.

John and Alan Lomax, a father and son team, have done many years of research in this field and have produced collections of folk-songs of all kinds. *American ballads and folk-songs* is a fairly typical example of their efforts, but individually and together they have made an impressive contribution to this area of the literature. *Folk-song U.S.A., Adventures of a ballad hunter* and *Folk-songs of North America* are all examples of their output. A very early collection of 136 *Slave songs of the United States* was published in 1867 by William Allen and others, and this has recently (1965) been re-issued with new piano accompaniments and guitar chords. Krehbiel's very important work *Afro-American folk-songs* was first published in 1914 and reprinted by Ungar in 1962. A special collection of one particular type of folk-song was produced by John Greenway in 1953. This was *American folk-songs of protest* published by the University of Philadelphia Press. Even more specialised is G. B. Johnson's *John Henry* which investigates the famous legend which has become one of the widest known of all Negro folk-songs. Another university press publication by Hans Nathan is *Dan Emett and the rise of the early Negro minstrelsy* published by the University of Oklahoma in 1962.

There are many other relevant titles in this field; for a further selection the reader is referred to the General Background section in Reisner's *Literature of jazz* or Haselgrove and Kennington's *Readers' guide to books on jazz,* 2nd ed. 1965.

The whole story of popular music in America in its widest interpretation has produced several substantial and well-written general histories. Probably the best is Gilbert Chase's monumental work *America's music*, of which the revised second edition appeared in 1967. In its 761 pages there are several individual chapters of direct interest to the jazz student; these are Chapter 21 (on ragtime) Chapter 22 (on the blues) and Chapter 23 (on the growth of jazz). This material is, of course, better covered elsewhere but the main value of this scholarly work is in its linking of jazz with the mainstream of American music. There is an extremely useful bibliography of 29 pages. Sigmund

Spaeth covers a narrower field which is clearly defined in the title *A history of popular music in America* (1948). This, too, has over 700 pages, of which the last 150 are devoted to detailed and extensive indexes and a bibliography. Two works by David Ewen which include similar material were published in 1957 and 1966. These are *Panorama of American popular music* and *American popular songs from the Revolutionary War to the present*.

Negro musicians and their music (1936) by Maud Cuney Hare covers all types of Afro-American performers to that date and Negro poet Langston Hughes published a much shorter work in 1955 called *Famous Negro music makers* in the same vein. This latter work is in the 'Famous biographies for young people' series.

Before coming to the more specific areas of pre-jazz material on which more detail can be included, one further book should be considered.

This is Henry Kmen's *Music in New Orleans* (1966) which is sub-titled 'the formative years 1791–1841'. It is a revised doctoral dissertation on the social history of white New Orleans music which contains some interesting material on the 'prehistoric' jazz era. In an excellent critical review of the book by Bruce King in *Jazz Monthly*, it is suggested that it helps to prove some of Blesh's theories (see Chapter 2). These imply that New Orleans jazz had a social origin in the racial discriminatory laws which forcibly integrated the Creole and free Negro communities with the poor former slaves after the Civil War. It helps to explain why jazz developed more rapidly and better in New Orleans than in other cities and it suggests that the unique part of the new music was part of the African musical tradition and not of European origin. It is thus a valuable and scholarly confirmation of theories which have been widely held but insufficiently proven.

The literature on the blues, and to a much lesser degree on gospel music and ragtime, is extremely valuable to the student of jazz. Much of the writing has a very considerable sociological content although that which is primarily of this nature will be considered separately later in this chapter. The work of the British authority Paul Oliver is very important in the literature of the blues. Oliver's four books, *Blues fell this morning* (1960), *Conversation with the blues* (1965), *Screening the blues* (1968) and *Story of the blues* (1969), are invaluable source material and were based on research done in extensive visits to the United States. The first volume uses 350 blues citations to show the life of the rural Negro and has chapters on work, gambling, travel, love, crime, etc. It is illustrated with extracts from the 'race' (Negro-aimed) catalogues of the record companies and is well documented with a full discography of quoted blues, an index of quoted blues singers and a four-page select bibliography. The main text of the second book, which is a sequel to the first, consists of verbatim extracts from the conversations the author had with 68 singers in 1960. Again it is well illustrated with 80 unusual photographs and in total is a valuable source book on its subject. In the third volume Oliver is chiefly concerned to interpret the blues enigma by explaining how a vocabulary of allusion, symbol and imagery carries code implication for the black audience and allows blues singers to get their songs on record and past the screen of white censorship.

Two earlier books on the blues were George Lee's *Beale Street, where the blues began,* which was published in 1934 and the Lomaxes' *Negro songs as sung by Leadbelly* (1936). The sub-title of this latter work describes succinctly the turbulent and influential life of Huddie Ledbetter, alias Leadbelly, in the following words: 'king of the twelve-string guitar players of the world, long-time convict in the penitentiaries of Texas and Louisiana.' An even earlier work by W. C. Handy and Abbe Niles (1926) contained the collected words and music of 67 blues songs together with an historical and critical text. This collection was issued under the title of *Blues* and re-published in 1949 as *A treasury of the Blues.* Handy's autobiography is mentioned in Chapter 3. Two other collections of blues compositions are Jerry Silverman's *Folk Blues* (1958) and Kay Shirley's *Book of the Blues* (1964). The latter was a joint effort; Shirley gave the music for some 100 items for the guitar, whilst discographical notes on each title and brief biographical details of each alleged composer were included by Frank Driggs,

Joy Graeme and Bob Hartsell. Harold Courlander's *Negro folk music U.S.A.* is a major and scholarly work which follows his *Haiti singing* (1939) and *The drum and the hoe* (1960). Together these (and other) books represent the result of thirty years' research into the Negro music of the Americas. *Negro folk music U.S.A.* is a serious, important book which collates into coherent form much of the diverse material written on this subject. Courlander is a strong supporter of the African roots theory but does not dispute the cultural blends. The chief criticism of the work is the lack of a recognisable chronology with the section on 'Blues' (perhaps the least convincing section), preceding 'Ring games and party songs', 'Louisiana Creole Songs', 'Ballads and minstrelsy' and 'Dances and Instruments'. Sections preceding the Blues are 'Anthems and Spirituals' and 'Sounds of work'. One feels the 'Blues' ought to have been dealt with towards the end of the book. Other University Press publications by Frederic Ramsey (*Been here and gone,* 1960) and Charles Keil (*Urban blues,* 1966) share the same subject interest and high standard. Keil particularly has produced a masterly work on a limited field with the theme that the urban blues is part of a valid, valuable and distinctly Negro culture. He is unusually well qualified to write his book since he is trained in the fields of musicology, anthropology and sociology, the understanding of all of which is vital to a balanced analysis of this musical culture. In addition he has worked as a practising jazz musician and thus brings authority of the highest order to this important document. Stanley Hyman's collection of essays and reviews *The promised end* (1963) includes a useful 20-page chapter on 'American Negro literature and the folk tradition' which includes a discussion of the relation of the blues to Negro literature.

Finally on the blues, there is the work of Samuel B. Charters. His *Country Blues* complements Keil's work and appeared originally in the United States in 1959. The English edition of 1960 included an extra appendix for British readers. The book is a mine of background information on the early country blues with much biographical detail on famous exponents of the art, such as Blind Lemon

Jefferson, Bill Broonzy, Leroy Carr, etc. It has some unusual illustrations, is the result of considerable original research and in total is a major source book for this branch of the subject. Other works by Charters are mentioned elsewhere in this Guide, but since his major interests are in this area it is appropriate to quote two further titles by him. These are *The poetry of the blues* (1963) and *The bluesmen* (1967).

Although many periodical articles have been written on ragtime over the years, only one complete book has appeared on the subject. This is accepted by most critics as the definitive work on the historical development and passing of true ragtime. Originally published in 1950, *They all played ragtime* by Rudi Blesh and Harriet Janis is subtitled 'the true story of an American music'. Because ragtime was so locally based in the mid-west and because it was a written music, as opposed to the usual improvised performances, it has tended to be rather unrecognised as an important precursor and ingredient of jazz itself. Blesh and Janis is a very important source book for information on Scott Joplin and his pianist colleagues and a comprehensive discography is included. The pioneer attempt at the musical analysis of ragtime by Guy Waterman was first published in the American jazz magazine *Record Changer* in the 1940's. This essay reappeared in a more permanent form in *The art of jazz* (1960) edited by Martin T. Williams. Ann Charters published a collection of ragtime pieces in 1965 under the title of *The ragtime songbook.* There is a brief introduction describing the ragtime era (approximately 1897–1917) with biographical notes on the leading musicians.

The final, and very important, group of works to be described in this chapter are the sociological writings on jazz and its background. The American Negro in general and the jazz musician in particular make excellent subjects for the sociologist. The reasons why this is so are fairly obvious: the transportation of a large number of people of a completely different racial and cultural background into the midst of a diverse mass of immigrants from a hostile Europe provides a rich field for sociological enquiry. In spite of the humane pretensions of white Americans, it seems that in only two areas is the Negro fully accepted as being equal and even superior to his white compatriots. One is in sport, in which Negro athletes and particularly boxers, have shown their prowess, and the second, which concerns this document, is in jazz. Undoubtedly the fact that the Negro 'invented' jazz music and developed it has been a source of pride for the coloured American. This is not to say that no white musician can really play jazz successfully, as is sometimes argued in extremist circles, but it cannot be denied that the major innovators have all been Afro-Americans. Louis Armstrong, Duke Ellington, and Charlie Parker all had completely different social backgrounds, their whole lives developed quite differently and their musical styles were disparate, but they were major figures in what is now recognised as a major musical stream. This preamble is designed to show that an understanding of the sociological background is vital to an understanding of jazz itself and we are lucky in having some excellent literary contributions to help in this. A study by Neil Leonard entitled *Jazz and the white Americans* explains the social and intellectual relationships of whites in America to a music associated primarily with the Negro. Leonard includes a 13-page bibliography in his book. From the other side of the colour line, Le Roi Jones, a leading Negro intellectual and poet, produced *Blues people: Negro music in white America* in 1963. This was a major contribution to the understanding of what jazz means to the educated Negro in particular and is worthy of close study. Jones, who has in recent years become increasingly involved in the militant Black Power movement, has also written a second book *Black music* which was published in 1967. Nat Hentoff, who has been author, or co-author, of several of the most worthwhile books on various aspects of jazz, has written *The new equality* and *The jazz life.* The latter is perhaps one of the few really indispensable jazz books and the author's main source of material is the talk of the musicians themselves. Hentoff manages to get them to talk freely and constructively about their music, their fellow musicians and the social background to their work and play. He gets the drugs problem into perspective too, but the book loses a little by having no index.

Britain's contribution to this area of the literature is a fine examination of the *Jazz scene* in 1959 by Frances Newton. This pseudonym hides the identity of a London University lecturer who also contributed pieces on jazz to the left-wing periodical *New Statesman.* Newton writes refreshingly and, although he claims to be no expert, probes deep into such interesting issues as the business world of jazz, the jazz public and the influence of jazz on 'serious' and 'popular' music. There is a detailed guide to sources at the end of the book which is very useful and the whole work is required reading for the jazz student. David Dachs' *Anything goes* (1964) is an analysis of the effect of the commercial world on popular music. Dachs includes jazz in his review.

The place of the gramophone in spreading the influence of jazz was mentioned earlier in the chapter. It seems, therefore, appropriate to conclude by mentioning two documents which cover the technical development of this invention. Roland Gelatt's *The fabulous phonograph* (1956) is a full length work presenting 'the story of the gramophone from tin foil to high fidelity'. More specific is Charles Graham's *Jazz and the phonograph* which was included in Leonard Feather's *New yearbook of jazz* (1959). This author combines expert knowledge of recording techniques and sound reproduction with an understanding of jazz music, and the resulting twelve-page essay is an outstanding contribution to this relatively neglected topic. Graham includes a brief chronology of recording from Edison in 1877 up to the widespread availability of stereophonic equipment in 1959. A brief 32-page pamphlet by Michael Wyler *A glimpse at the past* (1957) is useful for information on some of the early record companies that were associated with jazz.

BIBLIOGRAPHY

ABRAHAMS, R. D. *Deep down in the jungle: Negro narrative folklore from the streets of Philadelphia.* Hatboro, Pa., Folklore Associates, 1964.
ALLEN, W. F., WARE, C. P. *and* GARRISON, L. M. *Slave songs of the United States.* New York, A. Simpson, 1867.
———— New York, P. Smith, 1929. (Reprint of 1867 edition.)
—— *Slave songs of the United States.* The complete original collection (136 songs) collected and compiled by William Francis Allen, Charles Pickard Ware and Lucy McKim Garrison in 1867 with new piano accompaniment and guitar chords by Irving Schein. New York, Oak Publications, 1965.
ASBURY, H. *The French quarter: an informal history of the New Orleans underworld.* New York, Knopf, 1936.
———— London, Jarrolds, 1937.
ASCH, M. *and* LOMAX, A. *eds. The Leadbelly songbook.* New York, Oak Publications, 1962.
AUSTIN, W. W. *Music in the 20th century: from Debussy thru' Stravinsky.* New York, Norton, 1966. Intelligent treatment of jazz in a general history of music. In the two chapters devoted to jazz, the author picks out major contributors such as Morton, Armstrong, Ellington and Parker for detailed analysis. Bibliography pages 552–662.
—— *Music in the 20th century: from Debussy to Stravinsky.* London, Dent, 1967.
BLESH, R. *O Susanna: a sampler of the riches of American folk music.* London, Evergreen Press, 1962. Musical score by Hermann Wilson.
BLESH, R. *and* JANIS, H. *They all played ragtime: the true story of an American music.* New York, Knopf, 1950. Detailed and unique record of the development and passing of ragtime. Includes discography.
—— —— London, Sidgwick and Jackson, 1958.
—— —— Rev. ed. New York, Grove Press, 1959.
The BLUES project: the sound. New York, McGraw-Hill, 1968.
CHARTERS, A. *ed. The ragtime songbook.* Songs of the ragtime era by Scott Joplin and others, with historical notes concerning the songs and the times. New York, Oak Publications, 1965.
CHARTERS, S. B. *The bluesmen: the story and the music of the men who made the blues.* New York, Oak Publications, 1967 (hardback and paperback editions). Vol. 1. The singers and

12   *The Literature of Jazz*

the styles from Mississippi, Alabama, and Texas up to the
Second World War with a brief consideration of some of the
traceable relationships between the blues and African song.
—*The country blues.* New York, Rinehart, 1959. Source book
for the early country blues which is well researched and has
some unusual illustrations.
—— —— London, M. Joseph, 1960. English edition includes an
extra appendix.
—— —— London, Jazz Book Club, 1961.
—— *The poetry of the blues.* New York, Oak Publications, 1963.
Photography by Ann Charters. Significant study of Negro
folk blues based on extensive research and field recording
activities. Includes much interpretative and explanatory
material on the words of blues songs.
CHASE, G. *America's music: from the pilgrims to the present,*
New York, McGraw-Hill, 1955. Popular music in America
which includes chapters of jazz interest.
—— —— 2nd ed. New York, McGraw-Hill, 1966.
—— —— —— London, McGraw-Hill, 1966.
COURLANDER, H. *The drum and the hoe: life and lore of the
Haitian people.* Berkeley and Los Angeles, University of
California Press, 1960. Includes 109 pages of native music.
—— *Haiti singing: with the airs of songs and with plates.* Chapel
Hill, University of North Carolina Press, 1939. Haitian folk
music.
—— *Negro folk music U.S.A.* New York and London, Columbia
University Press, 1963. Serious work which brings together
much diverse material on its subject.
—— —— London, Jazz Book Club, 1966.
CUNARD, N. *Comp. Negro anthology, 1931–1933.* London,
Wishart and Co., 1934.
DACHS, D. *Anything goes: the world of popular music.* Indiana-
polis and New York, Bobbs-Merrill, 1964. Includes a chapter
on jazz.
DAVIS, J. P. *ed. The American Negro reference book.* Englewood
Cliffs, N.J., Prentice-Hall, 1966. Covers all aspects of Negro
life and useful as general background material.
ELKINS, S. M. *Slavery: a problem in American institutional and
intellectual life.* Chicago, Chicago University Press, 1959.
—— —— London, Cambridge University Press, 1960.
—— —— New York, Grosset and Dunlap, 1963. (Paperback ed.)
EWEN, D. *ed. American popular songs; from the Revolutionary
War to the present.* New York, Random House, 1966.

—— *Panorama of American popular music: the story of our national ballads, and folk songs, the songs of Tin Pan Alley, Broadway and Hollywood, New Orleans jazz, swing and symphonic jazz.* Englewood Cliffs, N.J., Prentice-Hall, 1957.

FINKELSTEIN, S. *Composer and nation: the folk heritage of music.* London, Lawrence and Wishart, 1960.

—— —— New York, International Publishers, 1960.

FISHER, M. M. *Negro slave songs in the United States.* Ithaca, N.Y., Cornell University Press for the American Historical Association, 1953.

—— —— London, Oxford University Press, 1954.

—— —— New York, Citadel Press, 1963. (Paperback ed.)

FRAZIER, E. F. *The Negro in the United States.* New York, Macmillan, 1949. Background reference work with full bibliography. Weak on musical aspects.

—— —— Rev. ed. New York, Macmillan, 1957.

GAMMOND, P. *and* CLAYTON, P. *A Guide to popular music.* London, Phoenix House, 1960. Covers the fields of popular song, dance music, folk music, etc.

—— *Dictionary of popular music* (originally titled *A guide to popular music*). New York, Philosophical Library, 1961.

GELATT, R. *The fabulous phonograph: from tin foil to high fidelity.* Philadelphia, Lippincott, 1955. A technical rather than an economic and social history.

—— —— *: the story of the gramophone from tin foil to high fidelity.* London, Cassell, 1956.

—— —— *: from Edison to stereo.* Rev. ed. New York, Appleton,1966.

GRAHAM, C. 'Jazz and the phonograph' (in FEATHER, L. *New yearbook of jazz,* London, A. Barker, 1959).

GREENWAY, J. *American folk songs of protest.* Philadelphia, University of Pennsylvania Press, 1953. Bibliography.

—— —— London, Oxford University Press, 1953.

HALL, S. *and* WHANNEL, P. *The popular arts.* London, Hutchinson Educational, 1964. Treats jazz intelligently in a wide ranging survey of popular arts. Shows contrast with 'pop' music and uses illustrations from jazz (as well as other arts) in suggesting new methods of communicating with young adults. Good annotated bibliography, of which pages 445–446 are devoted to jazz.

—— —— New York, Pantheon Books, 1965.

HANDY, W. C. *and* NILES, A. *Blues: an anthology.* New York, Boni, 1926. Traces the development of the most spontaneous and appealing branch of Negro folk blues to modern jazz.

—— *A treasury of the blues: complete words and music of the great songs from Memphis Blues to the present day.* (Originally published as *Blues: an anthology . . .*) New York, Boni, 1949. Historical and critical text by Niles.

HARE, M. C. *Negro musicians and their music.* Washington, Associated Publishers, 1936. Traces African beginnings through Afro-American folk-songs both religious and secular to a rather confined chapter on 'Negro idiom and rhythm' which covers the blues, ragtime and jazz itself. All this of interest to the jazz student as is the 26-page appendix on 'African musical instruments'. Remainder of the book is devoted to 'straight' musicians including some non-Americans.

HENTOFF, N. *The jazz life.* New York, Dial Press, 1961. Readable and lucid sociological approach based on discussions with musicians.

—— —— London, Peter Davies, 1962.

—— —— London, Hamilton, 1964 (Paperback ed.)

—— *The new equality.* New York, Viking Press, 1964.

—— —— Rev. ed. New York, Viking Press, 1965.

HOLLANDER, B. *Slavery in America: its legal history.* London, Bowes & Bowes, 1962 (verso of title page bears imprint 'Putnam & Co. London').

—— —— New York, Barnes & Noble, 1963.

HUGHES, L. *Famous Negro music-makers.* New York, Dodd, Mead, 1955. For children.

—— —— —— 1957.

HUGHES, L. *and* METZNER, M. *Black magic: a pictorial history of the Negro in American entertainment.* New York, Prentice-Hall, 1967.

HUSTON, J. *Frankie and Johnny.* New York, Boni, 1930. 'An adaptation for the stage of the song "Frankie & Johnny" based on the many versions which Mr. Huston has discovered throughout the country. Twenty of these versions appear at the back of the book together with a note on the St. Louis one, "Frankie & Albert" which is the most authentic.'

HYMAN, S. E. *The promised end: essays and reviews 1942–1962.* Cleveland and New York, World Publishing Co., 1963. Includes 20-page chapter on 'American Negro literature and the folk tradition'.

JOHNSON, G. B. *John Henry: tracking down a Negro legend.* Chapel Hill, University of North Carolina Press, 1929. Covers the story behind the Negro folk-song.

—— —— London, Oxford University Press, 1929.

JONES, A. M. *Studies in African music.* 2 volumes. London and New York, Oxford University Press, 1959.

JONES, L. *Black music.* New York, Morrow, 1967. Collection of essays on modern jazz black musicians, 1959–1966. Has much sociological content and has, according to one critic, 'enormous value quite apart from the light it throws on jazz . . . lets you know what it has felt like at various times to be a Negro in the United States.'

—— —— London, MacGibbon and Kee, 1969.

—— *Blues people: Negro music in white America.* New York, Morrow, 1963. Important book by leading Negro intellectual.

—— —— London, MacGibbon and Kee, 1965.

—— —— New York, Apollo editions, 1965. (Paperback ed.)

—— —— London, Jazz Book Club, 1966.

JONES, M. ed. *Folk: review of people's music.* London, Jazz Music Books, 1945.

KEIL, C. *Urban blues.* Chicago and London, Chicago University Press, 1966. Scholarly approach to the subject of city blues.

KENNEDY, R. E. *Mellows: a chronicle of unknown singers.* New York, Boni, 1925. Negro work songs, street cries and spirituals.

—— *More mellows.* New York, Dodd, Mead, 1931.

KING, B. 'The formative years', *Jazz Monthly,* v. 13 (6), 1967, pp. 5–7. Review of Kmen's *Music in New Orleans.*

KMEN, H. *Music in New Orleans: the formative years, 1791–1841.* Baton Rouge, Louisiana State University Press, 1967. Revised doctoral dissertation on the social history of white New Orleans music.

KREHBIEL, H. E. *Afro-American folk songs: a study in racial and national music (with musical notes).* New York and London, Schermer, 1913.

—— —— New York, Ungar, 1962.

LAMBERT, C. *Music ho!: a study of music in decline.* London, Faber, 1934. Refers to the work of jazz musicians without seeing the essence of jazz music.

—— —— Rev. ed. London, Faber, 1938.

—— —— London, Penguin Books in association with Faber, 1948. (Paperback ed.)

—— —— 3rd ed. London, Faber, 1966.

LEE, G. W. *Beale Street, where the blues began.* New York, R. O. Ballou, 1934.

LEONARD, N. *Jazz and the white Americans: the acceptance of a*

new art form. Chicago and London, Chicago University Press'
1962. Important study. Bibliography pages 193–206.
—— —— London, Jazz Book Club, 1964.
LOMAX, A. *Penguin book of American folk songs.* London,
Penguin Books, 1966.
—— comp. *The folk songs of North America.* London, Cassell,
1960.
LOMAX, J. arr. *Folksong U.S.A., the 111 best American ballads,*
edited by Alan Lomax. New York, Duell, Sloan and Pearce,
1947.
LOMAX, J. *and* LOMAX, A. *Adventures of a ballad hunter.* New
York, Macmillan, 1947. Autobiographical reminiscences.
—— *American ballads and folksongs.* New York, Macmillan, 1934.
Covers the whole range of American songs with words and
music. Particularly interesting sections are the Chain gang
songs (Chapter 3), Negro bad men (4), The blues (8), Creole
Negroes (9) and Negro spirituals (25).
—— eds. *The Leadbelly legend : a collection of world-famous songs
by Huddie Ledbetter.* Music edited by Hally Wood. New York,
Folkways Music Publishers, 1959. Words and music with
brief introductory matter.
—— —— 2nd ed. revised. New York, Folkways Music Publishers,
1965.
—— *Negro songs as sung by Leadbelly : king of the twelve-string
guitar players of the world, long-time convict in the penitentiaries
of Texas and Louisiana.* New York, Macmillan, 1936.
LONGSTREET, S. *Sportin' House : a history of the New Orleans
sinners and the birth of jazz.* Los Angeles, Sherbourne Press,
1965. Social background to early jazz which is superficial and
jejune.
MANNIX, D. P. *and* COWLEY, M. *Black cargoes : a history of the
Atlantic Slave Trade, 1518–1865.* New York, Viking Press, 1962.
—— —— London, Longmans, 1963.
—— —— New York, Viking Press, 1965. (Paperback ed.)
MILLER, W. R. *The world of pop music and jazz.* St. Louis, Mo.,
Concordia, 1965 (Christian encounters series).
NATHAN, H. *Dan Emett and the rise of early Negro minstrelsy.*
Norman, Okla., University of Oklahoma, 1962.
NETTL, B. *Folk and traditional music of Western continents.*
Englewood Cliffs, N.J., and London, Prentice Hall, 1965.
(Hard and paperback eds.)
NEWTON, F. *pseud. The jazz scene.* London, MacGibbon and
Kee, 1959.

—— —— London, Jazz Book Club, 1960.
—— —— New York, Monthly Review Press, 1960.
—— —— London, Penguin Books, 1961. (Paperback ed.)
ODUM, H. W. *and* JOHNSON, G. B. *The Negro and his songs: a study of typical Negro songs in the South.* Chapel Hill, University of North Carolina Press, 1925. (University of North Carolina Social Study Series.)
—— —— Hatboro, Pa., Folklore Associates, 1964. (Reprint of 1925 ed.)
—— *Negro workaday songs: with musical notes and a bibliography.* Chapel Hill, University of North Carolina Press, 1926. (University of North Carolina Social Study Series.)
—— —— London, Oxford University Press, 1926.
OLIVER, P. *Blues fell this morning: the meaning of the blues.* London, Cassell, 1960. Well documented scholarly work.
—— —— New York, Horizon Press, 1961.
—— *The meaning of the blues.* New York, Collier Books, 1963. (Paperback edition of *Blues fell this morning.*)
—— *Conversation with the blues.* London, Cassell, 1965. Valuable source book which supplements *Blues fell this morning.*
—— —— New York, Horizon Press, 1965.
—— —— London, Jazz Book Club, 1967.
—— *Screening the blues.* London, Cassell, 1968.
—— *Story of the blues.* London, Barrie and Rockliff, 1969.
RAMSEY, F. *Been here and gone.* Brunswick, N.J., Rutgers University Press, 1960. Useful and authoritative book.
—— —— London, Cassell, 1960.
—— —— London, Jazz Book Club, 1962.
—— *Chicago documentary: portrait of a jazz era.* London, Jazz Sociological Society, 1944.
ROUTLEY,E. *Is jazz music Christian?* London,Epworth Press,1964.
SCARBOROUGH, D. *On the trail of Negro folklore.* Hatboro, Pa., Folklore Associates, 1963.
SCARBOROUGH, D. *and* GULLEDGE, O. L. *On the trail of Negro folk-songs.* Cambridge, Mass., Harvard University Press, 1925.
—— —— Hatboro, Pa., Folklore Associates, 1963. (Facsimile rep. of 1925 ed.)
SHELTON, R. *and* RAIM, W. *The Josh White song book.* Chicago, Quadrangle Books, 1963. (Hardback and paperback eds.) Life story of singer Josh White together with simple arrangements of work songs and blues associated with the singer. Discography of American recordings.

—— —— London, Elek Books, 1964.

SHIRLEY, K. *The book of the blues.* New York, Crown Publishers, 1964. 100 pieces for the guitar together with notes on recordings and composers.

SILVERMAN, J. ed. *Folk blues.* New York, Macmillan, 1958. Arrangements for the guitar.

—— —— New York, Macmillan, 1967.

SPAETH, S. G. *A history of popular music in America.* New York, Random House, 1948. Fascinating background book on American popular songs up to 1948. Many of the songs quoted have been given jazz treatment and some have become 'classics' or 'standards'.

—— —— London, Phoenix House, 1960.

—— —— London, Jazz Book Club, 1962.

STAMPP, K. M. *The peculiar institution: slavery in the Ante-Bellum South.* New York, Knopf, 1956. Well documented and readable account of slavery in America.

—— —— London, Eyre & Spottiswoode, 1964.

—— —— New York, Vintage, 1964. (Paperback ed.)

TRIBUTE to Huddie Ledbetter. (Gen. editors Max Jones and Albert McCarthy. London, Jazz Music Books, 1946.

WATERMAN, G. 'Ragtime' (*in* WILLIAMS, M. T. ed. *The art of jazz: essays on the nature and development of jazz.* New York, Oxford University Press, 1959.)

WHITE, N. L. *American Negro folk-songs.* Cambridge, Mass., Harvard University Press, 1928. Important work with extensive bibliography.

—— —— Hatboro, Pa., Folklore Associates, 1965.

WORK, J. W. ed. *American Negro songs and spirituals: a comprehensive collection of 230 folk songs, religious and secular.* New York, Crown Publishers, 1940. Mainly words and music with five short introductory chapters on the 'Origins', 'The spiritual', 'The blues', 'Work songs' and 'Social and miscellaneous'. Useful brief bibliography listing 47 references.

—— —— New York, Howell, Soskin & Co., 1940.

—— *Folk song of the American Negro.* Nashville, Tenn., Fisk University Press, 1915.

WYLER, M. *A glimpse at the past: an illustrated history of some early record companies that made jazz history.* West Moors, Dorset, Jazz Publications, 1957.

CHAPTER 2

THE HISTORIES OF JAZZ

Jazz proper arose around the beginning of this century and, as is well known, New Orleans, Louisiana, was its cradle. This statement is no doubt a romantic oversimplification, but nevertheless the 'Crescent City', as it was known colloquially, had a vital part to play in early jazz development. The early street bands who played music for dancing at local functions were major pioneers, and the spread of the music did not really gather impetus until the second decade of the century. The development of the record industry at this time and the subsequent growth of radio broadcasting were the most important factors in the beginnings of what became a world-wide movement. The Original Dixieland Jazz Band is credited with having been the first to make gramophone records of jazz in 1917. This group of white imitators achieved world-wide fame because of this lucky chance and attained an importance out of all proportion to their talents. This saga is well documented in H. O. Brunn's *Story of the Original Dixieland Jazz Band* which was published in 1960. The putting down on paper of jazz history did not begin for many years and much historical writing is inevitably interlaced with analytical discussion of the music. This causes some problems in a work such as this one but the topics are dealt with in this and following chapters.

There seems little point in dealing with jazz histories chronologically, i.e. in the order in which they were published; it appears better to group them into those which cover the whole field in an unbiased way before dealing with those which cover certain periods or styles only, or projecting the history from a narrow base, or cover the progress of jazz in a certain country or geographical area.

Of the comprehensive histories the work of Professor Marshall Stearns is outstanding. His *Story of jazz* is a major work of scholarship, thoroughly researched and documented. Stearns, who published the original edition in the mid-1950's, was the founder of the Institute of Jazz Studies in New York (see Chapter 9) and was connected with it until his death in 1966. His contribution to the literature of jazz, and his efforts to elevate it to a subject worthy of independent study, were extremely important. *The story of jazz* covered all aspects of the music in a broad-minded, mature fashion and ran to several editions (including one in paperback). An extensive bibliography by Robert G. Reisner and a syllabus of 15 lectures on the history of jazz were included in the last edition. An earlier book by jazz critics Frederic Ramsey and Charles Smith appeared in 1939. This was *Jazzmen,* probably the first intelligent full-length appraisal to appear. It was particularly interesting to the historian because it contains some accurate assessments based on data collected by the authors and is therefore a contrast to the well-meaning but sometimes inaccurate commentaries of the pioneer European critics. A useful chapter on record collecting (by Stephen Smith) and 'Consider the critics' (by R. P. Dodge) are also included. The latter discusses the early written references to jazz in the periodical literature of the 1920's. Undoubtedly Ramsey and Smith's work is a watershed in jazz literature in that it provoked and inspired many of the subsequent books. No chapter on the history of jazz would be complete without reference to the work of the prolific French critic, Hugues Panassie. His books on analysis and criticism, biography and in the reference field appear in various chapters of this work, but much of his effort has gone into recording historical data. *Histoire du vrai jazz* (1959) is a typical title but there are several others which are listed at the end of this chapter. Panassie's earlier books, like those of all the European critics writing at the time, are not always as strictly accurate as they might be owing to the difficulty in locating relevant source material. The main value of this early work was its important role in making jazz respectable—that is a subject worthy of being written about.

The Belgian lawyer, Robert Goffin, also made numerous contributions to the literature of jazz between 1921 (*Jazz band*) and 1948 (*Nouvelle histoire du jazz, du Congo au bebop*). All of these were originally published in French and only his biography of Louis Armstrong *Horn of plenty* and *Jazz from the Congo to the Metropolitan* were translated into English. This latter work, which was titled *Jazz from Congo to Swing* in its British edition, deals in an informed way with early jazz and, unlike some other early books, had a strong confidence in jazz's future. The English edition was widely read and very influential just after the Second World War when very little jazz literature in book form was available. Goffin's *Aux frontières du jazz* (1932) was lacking in accuracy but was nevertheless an important landmark in getting the history of jazz into documentary form.

A group of books possessing many similarities appeared in the period between 1924 and 1934. They claimed to be serious works on the history and development of jazz and three of them included the word in their titles. All have interest to the jazz historian since they show how difficult it was for critics of that period to understand what it was they were trying to describe. Gilbert Seldes' *Seven lively arts* appeared in 1924 and was followed in 1926 by another American book *So this is jazz* by Henry Osgood. Osgood's book contains some interesting material but has many weaknesses since it concentrates on the work of dance band musicians who have since proved to have had little or no influence on the development of jazz. Osgood showed no faith in the future of what he regarded as jazz and was obsessed with the necessity for jazz to become 'respectable' in the manner of George Gershwin and others. He also appears to be the only work read by Percy Scholes and this—as is mentioned in Chapter 5—provides the basis for the almost useless article in the 1954 edition of the *Oxford companion to music.* On this side of the Atlantic, and consequently even further from the roots and origins of jazz, R.W.S. Mendl and Stanley Nelson offered their contributions to the literature. Mendl's *The appeal of jazz* (1927) is of limited value and the main aim of the author is to try and place jazz in the mainstream of music. Since Mendl was totally lacking in information on the work of major musicians like Oliver, Armstrong, etc., this was an impossible task. The result is a volume on jazz comparable to a book on 'serious' music with no mention of Bach, Beethoven and Mozart. *All about jazz* (1934) by Stanley Nelson concentrates on the activities of English musicians of the early 1930's. It is of little value except in its revelation of the attitudes of the supposedly well-informed music critics of the period.

A reliable history which does not, unlike some others, concentrate on the early history at the expense of later eras is Barry Ulanov's *History of jazz in America* which was published in 1952. Orrin Keepnews and Bill Grauer produced a *Pictorial history of jazz* in 1955 which is a 'tour-de-force' photographically; this was revised by Keepnews for a new edition which appeared in 1966. Shapiro and Hentoff's *Hear me talkin' to ya* has been referred to as the best single book on the subject and is the story of jazz as told by the men who made it. It is not an attempt to duplicate any of the formal histories but it does complement exceedingly well the work of Stearns and others. It is arranged chronologically and is recognised as a major source for historical information on jazz. The original edition of the work appeared in 1955, and there has been both a paperback and Book Club edition since then.

The work of Rudi Blesh has already been mentioned in the first chapter of this work but his major contribution to the literature of jazz is *Shining trumpets* which first appeared in 1946 and subsequently in further editions up to 1958. Blesh has a fine enthusiasm for the earlier period of traditional jazz and this book exerted wide influence when it first appeared. Because Blesh stubbornly refused to acknowledge the mainstream and modern schools, his reputation suffered among many enthusiasts in the 1950's. Now that his work can be seen in perspective, and also because many of his conclusions on the African roots of jazz have tended to be confirmed by uncommitted scholarly authors, his place as a writer of importance in jazz history seems to be assured. *Shining trumpets* is well documented and has extensive appendices which include a discography and 48 musical examples. Blesh was a constant propagandist for his view of jazz and through broadcasts and lectures did much to present it to a wider public. *This is jazz*, a pamphlet published in 1946, was a series of lectures given by him at the San Francisco Museum of Art. Less widely read, but nevertheless influential in Britain in the 1950's, was British critic Rex Harris. His original paperback *Jazz* first appeared in 1952 and ran to five editions before 1957. This book is good on the roots of jazz but his work generally needs to be approached with caution owing to his narrow view of the subject. A much broader view, completely without prejudice, is taken in Gunther Schuller's book *Early jazz* (1968). This volume has been described by one critic as being 'among the two or three finest contributions to jazz literature' and in it the author describes and analyses the music of the early jazz musicians up to 1930. Schuller, who is an academically trained musician and composer, offers the best interpretation yet of the African elements in jazz. In style he is the same mould as Andre Hodeir (see Chapter 4) and he has been known in the jazz world for some dozen years for his attempts to blend jazz and classical forms into Third Stream music. In this book, which is the first of two proposed, Schuller traces in detail the amalgamation of ragtime with early jazz, the emergence of Armstrong as a major soloist and of Morton as the first composer. He also covers Ellington's early work in depth and reinstates various unfairly neglected recordings and performers. The book is based solely on recordings.

Three volumes which cover the era of the big swing bands were published in middle 1960's. Leo Walker's *The wonderful era of the great dance bands* covers in its 315 pages the period 1925–1945 and gives details, with illustrations, of the work of Whiteman, Goldkette, Goodman, Dorsey, etc. It also includes the work of non-jazz orchestras. Gene Fernett's *A thousand golden horns* is half the length of the previous book and deals with the ten years between 1935 and 1945. All the main bands are covered but particularly valuable is the information on the lesser known orchestras of those years which often featured famous jazz musicians of all styles. Better than either of these is George Simon's *The big bands.* Simon's book is remarkable in its scope and shows clearly, though in a gossipy style, how deeply the big bands shaped a whole generation of popular and jazz musicians in the 'twenties, 'thirties and 'forties. He includes profiles of 72 major bands of the era and shorter biographies of over 300 less important orchestras. There are plenty of anecdotes but also many useful facts and interesting photographs.

A valuable work of reference on a specialised area of jazz history is Charters' and Kunstadts' *Jazz: a history of the New York scene.* As the sub-title indicates, this detailed and scholarly book confines itself to the developments in jazz in New York from 1920 to 1962. This book, too, is good on the big bands of the 'swing' era. A series of books under the general title of the Macmillan jazz masters series is edited by Martin Williams, a leading American critic. Somewhat uneven in quality, they are nevertheless a most useful summary of the various periods of jazz history. The basic approach is by brief essays on the work of the major figures of the period. These could in fact be viewed as collective biographies and therefore be quoted in the next chapter, but since they give a vivid picture of the various periods they have been included here. Titles so far published are *Jazz masters of the Fifties* by Joe Goldberg and *Jazz masters of the Forties* by Ira Gitler (both 1965), *Jazz masters of the Twenties* by Richard Hadlock (1966) and *Jazz masters of New Orleans* by the series editor Williams in 1967.

A substantial collection of essays of a high standard dealing with the history of jazz was published by Nat Hentoff and Albert J. McCarthy in 1959. This was *Jazz: new perspectives on the history of jazz*, in which the essays were written by twelve of the world's foremost jazz critics and scholars. Typical of the collection, and perhaps the most interesting, are Ernest Bornemann on 'The roots of jazz', Gunther Schuller on 'The Ellington style', Guy Waterman on 'Ragtime', and Franklin S. Driggs on 'Kansas City and the Southwest'. A very full list of recommended records covering all styles of jazz, blues and African music is included in the 387 pages.

The documentation of the history of jazz in individual

countries outside the United States has been attempted in a number of cases and complete books have resulted on occasions. David Boulton's *Jazz in Britain* (1958) is a disappointing early attempt to cover the whole field of British jazz with many major omissions and too much space allocated to relatively unimportant matters. From the continent of Europe there is Robert Pernet's *Jazz in little Belgium* which appeared in 1967. This work took six years to prepare and is obviously of importance in the documentation of European jazz, but it is spoilt by being physically of poor quality and also by the irritating manner in which it changes language from French to English and back again. There appears to be no discernible pattern at times. The book includes 338 pages of discography (out of 518 pages) of all jazz records by or with Belgian musicians. There is also a bibliography of some 90 books (divided into 'background books' and 'jazz books') and 20 jazz periodicals. Germany is served even better by critic Horst Lange and his *Jazz in Deutschland* is the definitive work on jazz in that country. Lange includes a comprehensive 5-page bibliography of the jazz literature in German; the list includes 23 journals. The same author has made major contributions to the discographical field and is referred to again in Chapter 5.

This concludes the description of the main histories of jazz music. The next chapter covers the personal histories of the important practitioners of the art.

BIBLIOGRAPHY

BLESH, R. *Shining trumpets: a history of jazz.* New York, Knopf, 1946. Good on early jazz but a controversial book owing to the author's prejudice against almost all post-1930 jazz.
—— —— London, Cassell, 1949.
—— —— 2nd ed. new and enlarged. New York, Knopf, 1958.
—— —— London, Cassell, 1958.
—— *This is jazz: a series of lectures given at the San Francisco Museum of Art.* San Francisco, The author, 1943.
—— —— London, Jazz Music Books, 1945.
BOULTON, D. *Jazz in Britain.* London, W. H. Allen, 1958.

26 *The Literature of Jazz*

—— —— Toronto, Smithers, 1958.

—— —— London, Jazz Book Club, 1960.

BRUNN, H. O. *The story of the Original Dixieland Jazz Band.* Baton Rouge, Louisiana State University Press, 1960. Detailed study of this pioneering white band.

—— —— London, Sidgwick and Jackson, 1961.

—— —— London, Jazz Book Club, 1963.

CHARTERS, S. B. *and* KUNSTADT, L. *Jazz: a history of the New York scene.* Garden City (N.Y.), Doubleday, 1962. Valuable work of reference on jazz in New York.

DEXTER, D. *Jazz cavalcade: the inside story of jazz.* New York, Criterion Press, 1946.

—— *The jazz story: from the 90's to the 60's.* Englewood Cliffs, N.J., Prentice-Hall, 1964. Superficial and written in poor journalese.

FERNETT, G. *Swing out: great Negro dance bands.* Midland, Mich., Pendell Co., 1970.

—— *A thousand golden horns: the exciting age of America's greatest dance bands.* Midland, Mich., Pendell Co., 1966. Covers the work of the big swing bands as well as some non-jazz orchestras for the period 1925–1945.

FOX, C. *Jazz in perspective.* London, British Broadcasting Corporation, 1969. Based on a series of excellent broadcasts on B.B.C. radio. Bibliography and discography pp. 81–88.

FRANCIS, A. *Jazz.* Paris, Editions du Seuil, 1958. (In French.) Includes discography and bibliography.

—— —— Translated and revised by Martin Williams. New York, Grove Press, 1960.

GAMMOND, P. *ed. The Decca book of jazz.* London, Muller, 1958. Contributions on a wide range of topics and musicians mainly by British authors. Discography.

GITLER, I. *Jazz masters of the forties.* New York, Macmillan, 1966. (Macmillan jazz masters series, edited by Martin Williams.) Not a great deal of new material but well put together. Covers the work of Parker, Gillespie, Bud Powell, J. J. Johnson, Oscar Pettiford, Kenny Clarke, Max Roach, Dexter Gordon, Lennie Tristano, Lee Konitz, Todd Dameron and other important instrumentalists of the decade.

GOFFIN, R. *Aux frontières du jazz.* Paris, du Sagittaire, 1932. (In French.) A major landmark in jazz documentation in spite of inaccuracies.

—— *Histoire du jazz.* Montreal, Parizeau, 1945. (In French.)

—— *Jazz 47.* Paris, Intercontinental du luxe, 1947. (In French.)

—— *Jazz, from the Congo to the Metropolitan.* Translated by Walter Schaap and Leonard G. Feather. New York, Doubleday, 1944. Interesting appraisal which was influential in the 1940's.

—— *Jazz, from Congo to swing.* Translated by Walter Schaap and Leonard Feather. London, Musicians Press, 1946 (originally titled *Jazz from the Congo to the Metropolitan*).

—— *Nouvelle histoire du jazz, du Congo au bebop.* Brussels, 'L'Ecran du monde', 1948. (In French.)

—— *La Nouvelle Orleans, capitale du jazz.* New York, La Maison francaise, 1946. (In French.)

GOLDBERG, J. *Jazz masters of the fifties.* New York, Macmillan, 1965. (Macmillan jazz masters series, edited by Martin Williams.) Journalistic in style and with no index or bibliography. Chapters on Gerry Mulligan, Thelonius Monk, Art Blakey, Miles Davis, Sonny Rollins, the Modern Jazz Quartet, Charles Mingus, Paul Desmond, Ray Charles, John Coltrane, Cecil Taylor and Ornette Coleman.

—— —— London, Collier-Macmillan, 1965.

GREEN, B. *Jazz decade: ten years at Ronnie Scott's.* London, Kings Road Publishing Ltd., 1969.

HADLOCK, R. *Jazz masters of the twenties.* New York, Macmillan, 1966. (Macmillan jazz masters, edited by Martin Williams.) Although no index is provided each chapter has a list of recommended books. Contains chapters on Louis Armstrong, Earl Hines, Bix Beiderbecke, the Chicagoans, Fats Waller, James P. Johnson, Jack Teagarden, Fletcher Henderson, Don Redman, Bessie Smith and Eddie Lang.

—— —— London, Collier-Macmillan, 1966.

HARRIS, R. *Jazz.* London, Penguin Books, 1952. Original paperback which is good on the roots of jazz and the traditional styles. Bibliography.

—— —— 2nd ed. London, Penguin Books, 1953.

—— —— 3rd ed. London, Penguin Books, 1954.

—— —— 4th ed. London, Penguin Books, 1956.

—— —— 5th ed. London, Penguin Books, 1957.

—— *The story of jazz* (abridged edition of *Jazz*). New York, Grosset and Dunlap, 1955.

—— —— New York, Grosset and Dunlap, 1960.

HENTOFF, N. *and* McCARTHY, A. J. *eds. Jazz: new perspectives on the history of jazz etc. by twelve of the world's foremost jazz critics and scholars.* New York, Rinehart, 1959. Substantial essays of a high standard and a very full list of recommended records covering all styles of jazz, blues and African music. *Contains* Ernest Borneman, 'The roots of jazz', pp. 1–20. Charles Edward Smith, 'New Orleans and the traditions in jazz', pp. 21–42. Guy Waterman, 'Ragtime', pp. 43–58. Martin Williams, 'Jelly Roll Morton', pp. 59–82. Paul Oliver, 'Blues to drive the blues away', pp. 83–104. Max Harrison, 'Boogie-woogie', pp. 105–136. John Steiner, 'Chicago', pp. 137–170. Hsio Wen Shih, 'The spread of jazz and the big bands', pp. 171–188. Franklin S. Driggs, 'Kansas City and the Southwest', pp. 189–230. Gunther Schuller, 'The Ellington style: its origins and early development', pp. 231–274. Max Harrison, 'Charlie Parker', pp. 275–286. Martin Williams, 'Bebop and after: a report', pp. 287–302. Albert J. McCarthy, 'The re-emergence of traditional jazz', pp. 303–324. Nat Hentoff, 'Whose art form? jazz at mid-century', pp. 325–342.

—— —— London, Cassell, 1960.

—— —— New York, Grove Press, 1961. (Paperback ed.)

—— —— London, Jazz Book Club, 1962.

HUGHES, L. *The first book of jazz.* New York, Watts, 1954 (for children).

—— —— 2nd ed. revised. London, Mayflower Press, 1962.

JONES, M. *Jazz photo album : a history of jazz in pictures.* London, British Yearbooks, 1947.

KEEPNEWS, O. *and* GRAUER, B. *Pictorial history of jazz : people and places from New Orleans to modern jazz.* New York, Crown Publishers, 1955. Good collection of photographs.

—— —— London, Hale, 1956.

—— —— ; revised by Orrin Keepnews. London, Spring Books, 1959.

—— —— 2nd ed. New York, Crown Publishers, 1966.

—— —— London, Spring Books, 1968.

LANGE, H. *Jazz in Deutschland.* Berlin, Colloquium Verlag, 1966. (In German.) Definitive work on German jazz history. Bibliography.

MENDL, R. W. S. *The Appeal of jazz.* London, P. Allan, 1927. First full-length book supposedly on jazz to be published in Great Britain. Author has little to say on any of the major jazz musicians and the main aim is to place the music of Whiteman, Ferdie Grofé *et al.* in the stream of 'serious' music.

NELSON, S. R. *All about jazz.* London, Heath, Cranton, 1934. Mainly covers the British jazz scene and dance music of the early 1930's. Little to do with the mainstream of jazz itself.

OSGOOD, H. O. *So this is jazz.* Boston, Little, Brown, 1926.

The Histories of Jazz   29

Early American book which totally fails to perceive the real significance of jazz. Unfortunately it formed the basis of Percy Scholes' article on jazz in the *Oxford Companion to Music.*

PANASSIE, H. *Cinq mois à New-York.* Paris, Correa, 1947. (In French.)

—— *Douze années de jazz (1927–1938) Souvenirs.* Paris, Correa, 1946. (In French.)

—— *Histoire du vrai jazz.* Paris, R. Laffont, 1959. (In French.) In many ways a restatement of his book *The real jazz* in which he shows his remoteness from the centre of creative jazz. His attitude towards the modern schools remains as hard as ever. Nevertheless Panassie is a major influence in jazz criticism.

—— *Quand Mezzrow enregistre: histoire des disques de Milton Mezzrow et Tommy Ladnier.* Paris, Laffont, 1952. (In French.) The story of a famous recording session in 1939.

PERNET, R. *Jazz in little Belgium: history (1881–1966), discography (1894–1966).* Bruxelles, Editions Sigma, 1967. (In French and English.)

POLILLO, A. *Conoscere il jazz.* Milan, Mondadori, 1967. (In Italian.)

—— *Jazz: a guide to the history and development of jazz and jazz musicians,* translated from the Italian by Peter Muccini. English edition edited by Neil Ardley. Feltham, Hamlyn, 1969.

RAMSEY, F. *and* SMITH, C. E. *eds. Jazzmen.* New York, Harcourt, Brace, 1939. Significant book of great importance in any study of jazz music.

—— —— London, Sidgwick and Jackson, 1957.

—— —— London, Jazz Book Club, 1958.

SCHULLER, G. *Early jazz: its roots and early development.* Volume 1. London and New York, Oxford University Press, 1968. First of two proposed volumes.

SELDES, G. V. *The seven lively arts.* London and New York, Harper, 1924. Treats jazz as if it consisted of Tin Pan Alley, Ragtime and the songs of Irving Berlin.

—— —— New York, Sagamore Press, 1957.

SHAPIRO, N. *and* HENTOFF, N. *eds. Hear me talkin' to ya: the story of jazz by the men who made it.* New York, Rinehart, 1955. Vital book for all jazz students.

—— —— London, Peter Davies, 1955.

—— —— London, Penguin Books, 1962. (Paperback ed.)

—— —— London, Jazz Book Club, 1967.
SIMON, G. T. *The big bands.* New York, Macmillan. London, Collier-Macmillan, 1967. An excellent guide to the work of the 'swing era' orchestras.
STEARNS, M. W. *The story of jazz.* New York, Oxford University Press, 1956. A major work of reference which is a basic textbook on the subject.
—— —— London, Sidgwick and Jackson, 1957.
—— —— ; with an expanded bibliography and a syllabus of fifteen lectures on the history of jazz. New York, New American Library, 1958.
—— —— London, Muller, 1958. (Paperback ed.)
ULANOV, B. *A history of jazz in America.* New York, Viking Press, 1952. A reliable historical text.
—— —— London, Hutchinson, 1958.
WALKER, L. *The wonderful era of the great dance bands.* Berkeley, Calif., Howell North, 1964.
WILLIAMS, M. T. *Jazz masters of New Orleans.* New York, Macmillan, 1967. (Macmillan jazz masters series, edited by Martin Williams.) Not a great deal of new information but the book does bring together in readable form much data on the major figures of New Orleans pioneering days. Each chapter has a brief discography and list of references. Chapters on Buddy Bolden, the Original Dixieland Jazz Band, Jelly Roll Morton, Joe 'King' Oliver, the New Orleans Rhythm Kings, Sidney Bechet, Louis Armstrong, Zutty Singleton, Kid Ory and Henry 'Red' Allen.
WOODWARD, W. *Jazz Americana : the story of jazz and all-time jazz greats from Basin Street to Carnegie Hall.* Los Angeles, Trend Books, 1956.

CHAPTER 3

THE LIVES OF JAZZMEN

Since jazz is so much a player's art, with composers, arrangers, music publishers and critics secondary figures, it seems to follow that the readers of jazz literature will be mainly interested in the lives of the practising jazzmen. This is in direct contrast to most other forms of music where the composer is the key figure. The jazz musician, his background and the influences both on him and by him are important to the connoisseur.

It should be made clear at this point that, apart from the autobiographies mentioned, the books quoted in this chapter are usually a mixture of biography and criticism— with varying discographical information being given. Thus there is considerable overlap between this chapter and the next one where analysis and criticism are considered. There are also a number of works in the biodiscography group which are dealt with in Chapter 5 along with other discographical literature. In this type of work the bulk of the volume is devoted to discography, although much substantial biographical detail is often included as in Allen and Rust's *King Joe Oliver.*

There is also obviously a close link between the general histories in Chapter 2 and the personal histories in this chapter. The author feels that it is useful to try and distinguish these two categories.

Since writing is not the jazzman's usual form of expression, many of the autobiographies have been produced by musicians with the aid of 'ghost' writers (usually journalists) and this does lead to some dilution in many, though not all cases, together with the undue emphasis which is often placed on sensational aspects of a musician's career. Doubtless the journalistic emphasis on prison sentences, drug addiction and the like gives the books an appeal to a slightly wider readership, but this journalistic flavour is often detrimental from a musicological point of view. The sociological studies mentioned in Chapter 1 put these problems in much better perspective.

There are several good examples of collective biography including Shapiro and Hentoff's *The jazz makers* (1957) and Robert Reisner's *The jazz titans* (1960) which includes 33 profiles of musicians. Collections of essays on modern jazz practitioners by Michael James (*Ten modern jazzmen* (1960)) and Raymond Horricks *et al.* (*These jazzmen of our time* (1959)) are also analytical and are referred to again in Chapter 4. The former analyses the recorded work of Charlie Parker, Dizzy Gillespie, Bud Powell, Miles Davis, Stan Getz, Thelonius Monk, Gerry Mulligan, John Lewis, Lee Konitz and Wardell Gray.

It would be difficult for any two jazz enthusiasts to agree on the five most important figures in jazz history but a personal list of Armstrong, Ellington, Parker, Basie and Morton, though controversial particularly in the last two named, would provide a basis for further discussion. In the jazz literature these men are documented fully. Louis Armstrong's progress from early New Orleans days has been recorded by himself in two books published in 1936 and 1954. *Swing that music,* the earlier of the two, was a brief record of his career to that date and apart from Paul Whiteman's *Jazz* (1926) was probably the first full-length jazz biography. In 1954 Armstrong (with journalistic aid undoubtedly) produced *Satchmo: my life in New Orleans* which was written in the racy style in which he speaks. This book is of interest because it clearly portrays the early life and background of Armstrong who is certainly one of the major figures in jazz. His influence is world-wide and has spanned several generations of musicians. Robert Goffin published a biography of Armstrong in French in 1947 and this was translated and published in the U.S.A. in the same year under the title *Horn of plenty.* Finally, a brief, but perhaps more objective, appraisal of Armstrong's career appeared in the Cassell Kings of Jazz series in 1960. It was by British critic Albert J. McCarthy and was entitled simply *Louis Armstrong.* Altogether 12 volumes appeared in this extremely useful series between 1959 and 1963. All were written by leading critics and the musicians covered range from Bessie Smith to Miles Davis, including such diverse artists as Duke Ellington, Dizzy Gillespie, Johnny Dodds and Coleman Hawkins. In short, the whole spectrum of jazz interest.

Apart from G. E. Lambert's contribution to the above-mentioned series on *Duke Ellington,* which deals concisely and well with the life and work of one of the great artists of the twentieth century, there are two earlier books on Ellington produced by Barry Ulanov (1946) and Peter Gammond (1958). Ulanov's work was also published in Spanish in Buenos Aires, Argentina, later that year. Gammond's collection of essays written by 14 critics assesses Ellington's contribution to jazz under four main headings. The first part covers the man himself and the second deals with his music in the successive decades from the 'twenties to the 'fifties, and with Ellington as a pianist and a composer. The third part covers the Ellington musicians and the fourth part is a discographical guide from 1926–1957.

Charlie Parker was responsible more than anyone else for the transition of some jazz in the early 1940's to the 'cool' style of modern jazz. Parker's life and work has inspired a number of books mainly because of its mixture of inspired genius, personal tragedy and brief span. Max Harrison wrote a brief book in the Kings of Jazz series in 1960, entitled *Charlie Parker,* and in 1962 a novel based on Parker's life was published. This was Ross Russell's *The sound* which will be mentioned again in Chapter 7 of this work. In 1963 Robert G. Reisner compiled and had published *Bird : the legend of Charlie Parker* which was a collection of articles, stories and random memories arranged in no special order and presented with a minimum of editing and correction—even obvious errors of fact are retained. This is, nevertheless, a vivid and vital picture of one of the greatest jazzmen of all time and the society in which he lived.

Count Basie and his orchestra, by Raymond Horricks

(1957), is the biography of a band, for Horricks appreciates that Basie can hardly be considered separately from his musicians. Individual pen portraits of the main musicians who have worked for Basie are included and the author tries hard to present his information without just listing titles of records and groups of musicians. There is a comprehensive discography by Alun Morgan which extends to almost 40 of the 320 pages.

Ferdinand 'Jelly Roll' Morton was a fascinating character whose colourful memories and boasts are beautifully documented by Alan Lomax in his *Mister Jelly Roll* which was originally published in 1950 and has since appeared in Book Club and paperback editions. Lomax, of the Library of Congress Folk Music Division, has been an indefatigable documentor of all types of North American folk music including jazz. This particular book stems from the recorded reminiscences of Morton just prior to the Second World War when he visited the Library of Congress over a period of days. Morton's musical career was at its lowest ebb and he was in a bitter mood but nevertheless the records made at this time have become of great importance in filling gaps in the history of jazz. Much of what was said has to be assessed with Morton's record as a braggart in mind, and his claims to have 'invented' jazz are ludicrous. In spite of this, the book is a great success since Lomax lets the colourful personality of Morton emerge and merely fills in the background himself. In the appendices are transcripts of several of Morton's piano pieces but unfortunately there is no index. A 40-page discography compiled by Thomas Cusack appeared as a separate pamphlet with the original edition of the book (see bibliography to Chapter 5 for details). Another brief, and rather more objective, life of *Jelly Roll Morton* was published by Martin T. Williams in the Kings of Jazz series in 1962.

Other literature which falls within the scope of this chapter can be very broadly sub-divided into groupings by style and/or periods as far as Americans are concerned with a final section on British and European musicians.

The blues, which is covered in Chapter 1, has produced some major figures but relatively few biographies of

individual artists. Although W. C. Handy was not a practitioner, he was closely linked with this area of jazz because
of his efforts to write down in terms of musical notation
what he heard around him in the Southern States. His
autobiography *Father of the blues*, which was published in
the U.S.A. in 1941, is of relevance to this section. Much
more down-to-earth are the stories of Perry Bradford and
William 'Big Bill' Broonzy. Bradford's *Born with the blues*
(1965) deals with the pioneering blues singers and is a
strident 'chip on the shoulder' book with interesting detail
of early jazz in New York. Broonzy's *Big Bill blues* originally
appeared in 1955 during its author's lifetime. It was written
in collaboration with the Belgian critic Yannick Bruynoghe
who published a completely revised edition in 1964, which
included a comprehensive discography of Broonzy's work.
The book is essential background reading for a real understanding of the life of the itinerant blues singer and the
development of the blues as a musical form.

A good example of the use of journalistic licence by
'ghost' writers mentioned earlier in this chapter is *Lady
sings the blues* (1958). This was written by Billie Holiday
shortly before her death, in collaboration with William Dufty
and stresses to the full the tragic circumstances and
sensational aspects of the singer's life. The important
musical aspects of her career are not well covered. One of
the better of the 'ghosts' was Bernard Wolfe who assisted
Milton Mezzrow, the clarinet player, to write his memoirs in
1946. The book *Really the blues* nevertheless dwells on
Mezzrow's spells in gaol on drug charges and is written in
a slangy style. A useful ten-page glossary of jazz terminology is included.

Lives of musicians belonging to the traditional and mainstream jazz schools are plentiful and vary greatly in quality
of contents. Sidney Bechet, a leading New Orleans Creole
musician, published his life-story *Treat it gentle* in 1960.
Bechet was a major influence on jazz clarinet and soprano
saxophone playing and his playing career lasted over forty
years. His last few years were spent in France where he
dominated the French traditional jazz world. The book,
which is an edited version of tape-recorded reminiscences,

includes a complete discography by David Mylne. Bechet's French connections are also reflected by a biography written in French by Raymond Mouly and published under the title *Sidney Bechet, notre ami* in 1961. A complete discography by Pierre Lafargue is included in this work.

Thomas 'Fats' Waller has also attracted several biographers including Charles Fox with *'Fats' Waller* (1960) and Ed. Kirkeby with *Ain't misbehavin'* (1966). Kirkeby was at one time Waller's manager and the book title is taken from one of the pianist's most famous compositions. Another natural for the biographer is Beiderbecke and here again (as in the case of Charlie Parker above) his life inspired the novelist. Dorothy Baker's *Young man with a horn,* which was the prototype jazz novel, appeared in 1938, eight years after the musician's death. This work is referred to again in Chapter 7. More factual accounts of Beiderbecke's work appear in *Bix Beiderbecke* by Burnett James (1959) and the sentimental *Bugles for Beiderbecke* (1958) by Wareing and Garlick. George Lewis, Eddie Condon, Max Kaminsky, King Oliver, Jack Teagarden and others have all written about themselves or have been written about and their stories are of varying degrees of interest to the jazz student and historian. Condon in *We called it music* provides interesting sidelights on the Chicago jazz scene of the 'twenties and 'thirties, and Kaminsky in *My life in jazz* also has some instructive things to say on the day-to-day life of a professional jazz musician. Kaminsky's musical work is not highly significant but the bulk of jazz is produced by solid musicians like him and it is therefore interesting to get his view. Another typical example of jazz autobiographical writing is *Music on my mind* by Willie 'The Lion' Smith. This is sub-titled 'the memoirs of an American pianist' and is hardly literature but it is full of interesting facts about various musicians met during 50 years playing experience. It is unusual, for this type of book, in having a very good index and some useful bibliographical and discographical information in the appendices.

The period 1935–1945 was the era of the big swing bands and two of the major band leaders of this time were Benny Goodman and Artie Shaw. Goodman's orchestra was a group of important musicians which has had tremendous influence both in the swing era and after. He was the first major band leader to front a mixed group of Negro and white musicians and this breakthrough on the social level, plus the superb orchestral arrangements used by the band, have ensured Goodman an important niche in jazz history. His autobiography *Kingdom of swing*, written with journalistic help at the height of his fame in 1939, does not reflect his musical importance. It was republished in paperback form in 1962 and gives some useful data on the 1930's, but it was sharply criticised by English critic Benny Green in his essay on Goodman included in *The reluctant art.* A lesser practitioner, both as a performer on the clarinet and rather more so as an organiser of successful big bands, was Artie Shaw. As a contributor to the literature of jazz, however, Shaw outshines Goodman, and his book *The trouble with Cinderella* shows that he was an intelligent man and an able writer. This makes his book worthy of some study since very few jazz musicians have had the ability to write as lucidly.

Apart from the books on Charlie Parker, musicians of the modern schools of jazz have not, in the main, been provided with full length biographies. This is not entirely surprising since most of them are still actively practising and a detached and objective assessment of their work is not very easy to make. A number of collections of biographical essays have appeared, such as Reisner's *The jazz titans* and in Cassell's 'Kings of Jazz' series brief volumes on Gillespie and Miles Davis contributed to knowledge on their lives and background. At the appropriate time major studies of this group of men will undoubtedly appear.

The final grouping of Americans which need to be dealt with in this chapter are the jazz-tinged popular artists. Such entertainers as Bing Crosby and Hoagy Carmichael have had close connections with jazz, and the musicians who play it over the years and their life stories have a direct bearing on the development of the music. Crosby, whose own book *Call me lucky* in 1953 followed Ted Crosby's *Story of Bing Crosby* (1946), was in his early days a singer with jazz bands like Eddie Condon's and he retained an affection for the music throughout his career. Hoagy Carmichael, songwriter and pianist, was a close friend of Beiderbecke and other Chicago-style musicians and a number of his tunes have become standards in the jazz-man's repertoire. *Sometimes I wonder* by Carmichael was written in 1965 and supplements *The stardust road* which appeared nearly 20 years earlier.

Negro women singers Lena Horne and Ethel Waters in their autobiographies also have something to say on the close links between the American show business set-up and the jazz world. The former has published *In person, Lena Horne* (1965) while Ethel Waters, who belonged to an earlier generation, told her story in *His eye is on the sparrow* (1951). Miss Waters, who began as a blues singer and ended her career mainly as an actress, provides some interesting fringe material on the jazz scene of the 'twenties and 'thirties.

The major European contributor to the development of jazz was probably the French gypsy guitarist Django Reinhardt. His work with colleagues in the Quintet of the Hot Club France produced what could be described as a European strain of jazz and his biography is therefore of unusual interest. Charles Delaunay's *Django Reinhardt* was originally published in French in 1954 and was not trans-lated into English until 1961. There is a comprehensive 78-page discography included in the book. A British pioneer was Spike Hughes, a highly literate man who, in the second volume of his autobiography *Second movement*, describes his deep involvement in British jazz around 1930. The book appeared in 1951 long after Hughes had severed all his connections with jazz but it is a fascinating and vital piece on the history of jazz on this side of the Atlantic. British jazz was also fortunate in that another highly literate musician appeared on the scene after the Second World War in the shape of trumpet-player Humphrey Lyttleton. Lyttleton's amusing and instructive books *I play as I please* and *Second chorus* document in an entertaining style the period 1945–1958 in British jazz history.

BIBLIOGRAPHY

Collective Biography
GRAHAM, A. P. *Strike up the band: bandleaders of today.* New York, Nelson, 1949.
HORRICKS, R. *and others. These jazzmen of our time.* London, Gollancz, 1959. Essays on modern jazz musicians.
JAMES, M. *Ten modern jazzmen: an appraisal of the recorded work of ten modern jazzmen.* London, Cassell, 1960. Collection of essays which analyses the recorded work of Charlie Parker, Dizzy Gillespie, Bud Powell, Miles Davies, Stan Getz, Thelonius Monk, Gerry Mulligan, John Lewis, Lee Konitz and Wardell Gray.
REISNER, R. G. *The jazz titans, including 'The parlance of hip'* with short biographical sketches and brief discographies.* Garden City, N.Y., Doubleday, 1960. 33 profiles.
SHAPIRO, N. *and* HENTOFF, N. *eds. The jazz makers.* New York, Rinehart, 1957.
—— —— New York, Grove Press, 1958. (Paperback edition.)
—— —— London, Peter Davies, 1958.
TERKEL, S. *Giants of jazz.* New York, Crowell, 1957. For younger readers.

Louis Armstrong (trumpeter, singer and bandleader)
ARMSTRONG, L. *Satchmo: my life in New Orleans.* New York, Prentice-Hall, 1954. Chiefly of interest because it clearly portrays the early life and background of one of the major figures in jazz. Takes Armstrong's career up to the time he left for Chicago in 1922 to join King Oliver's band.
—— —— London, Peter Davies, 1955.
—— —— New York, Signet, 1955. (Paperback edition.)
—— —— London, Jazz Book Club, 1957.
—— *Swing that music.* London, Longmans, 1936. Music section edited by Horace Gerlach.
EATON, J. *Trumpeter's tale: the story of young Louis Armstrong.* New York, Morrow, 1955 (for children).
GOFFIN, R. *Horn of plenty: the story of Louis Armstrong.* Translated by James Bezou. New York, Allen, Towne and Heath, 1947.
—— *Louis Armstrong, le roi du jazz.* Paris, P. Seghers, 1947. (In French.)
McCARTHY, A. J. *Louis Armstrong.* London, Cassell, 1960. (Kings of jazz series no. 5.)

—— —— New York, Barnes, 1961.
PANASSIE, H. *Louis Armstrong.* Paris, Le Belvedere, 1947. (Les maitres du jazz vol. 1.) (In French.)

William 'Count' Basie (pianist and bandleader)
HORRICKS, R. *Count Basie and his orchestra: its music and musicians.* London, Gollancz, 1957. The biography of the Basie band—both in total and of individual musicians. There is a comprehensive discography by Alun Morgan.
—— —— London, Jazz Book Club, 1958.

Sidney Bechet (soprano saxophonist and clarinettist)
BECHET, S. *Treat it gentle.* New York, Hill and Wang, 1960. Complete discography by David Mylne. The autobiography of a leading New Orleans Creole musician edited from tape-recorded reminiscences. Bechet was a major influence on jazz clarinet and soprano saxophone playing and played with many other prominent jazzmen in his career which spread over 40 years.
—— —— London, Cassell, 1960.
—— —— London, Jazz Book Club, 1962.
—— —— London, Transworld, 1964. (Paperback edition.)
MOULY, R. *Sidney Bechet, notre ami.* Paris, La Table Ronde, 1959. Complete discography by Pierre Larargue. (In French.)

Leon 'Bix' Beiderbecke (cornetist)
JAMES, B. *Bix Beiderbecke.* London, Cassell, 1959. (Kings of jazz series no. 4.) Concise and easy-to-read with fact separated from legend.
—— —— New York, Barnes, 1961.
WAREING, C. H. *and* GARLICK, G. *Bugles for Beiderbecke.* London, Sidgwick and Jackson, 1958. A sentimental view of the Beiderbecke legend.

Bernard 'Acker' Bilk (clarinettist and bandleader)
LESLIE, P. *and* GWYNN-JONES, P. *Book of Bilk.* London, MacGibbon & Kee, 1961.
—— —— London, Jazz Book Club, 1963.

Perry Bradford (blues singer)
BRADFORD, P. *Born with the blues: the true story of the pioneering blues singers and musicians in the early days of jazz.* New York, Oak Publications, 1965. (Paperback edition 1966.)

William 'Big Bill' Broonzy (blues singer)
BROONZY, W. *and* BRUYNOGHE, Y. *Big Bill: mes blues, ma
guitare et moi. Recits recueillis par Yannick Bruynoghe.* Pref. de
Hughes Panassie. Brussels, Editions des Artistes, 1955.
—— —— *Big Bill blues: William Broonzy's story as told to Yannick
Bruynoghe.* London, Cassell, 1955. Brief 'ghosted' biography
which fills in the background to the lives of rural blues singers.
Essential background reading for a real understanding of the
origins of jazz and the development of the blues. Line drawings
by Paul Oliver and discography by Albert McCarthy.
—— —— London, Jazz Book Club, 1957.
BRUYNOGHE, Y. *Big Bill blues.* 2nd. ed. New York, Oak Publications, 1964. This edition completely revised after Broonzy's
death with a complete new discography. (Hardback and
paperback editions.)

Hoagy Carmichael (pianist and composer)
CARMICHAEL, H. *and* LONGSTREET, S. *Sometimes I wonder:
the story of Hoagy Carmichael.* New York, Farrar, Straus and
Giroux, 1965. Life of a leading singer, composer and pianist
who was involved in Chicago-style jazz with Beiderbecke in
his younger days.
—— —— London, Redman, 1966.
CARMICHAEL, H. *The stardust road.* New York, Rinehart, 1946.
—— —— London, Musicians Press, 1947.

Eddie Condon (guitarist and bandleader)
CONDON, E. *and* SUGRUE, T. *We called it music: a generation of
jazz.* New York, Holt, 1947. A descriptive piece on the pro-
hibition era and in particular on the white Chicago-style
musicians of that time. Condon has impressed his own style
on much of this music and has therefore exerted more influence than his own musical talents warranted. A useful and
interesting book with a 22-page discography by John Swingle.
—— *We called it music: a generation of jazz.* London, Peter
Davies, 1948.
—— —— London, Jazz Book Club, 1956.
—— —— London, Corgi Books, 1962. (Paperback edition.)

Bing Crosby (singer)
CROSBY, B. *and* MARTIN, P. *Call me lucky.* New York, Simon
and Schuster, 1953. Crosby's main fame as a popular singer

was preceded by a close involvement in the jazz world of the
late 1920's and early 1930's and thus his biography is relevant.
—— —— London, Muller, 1953.
CROSBY, E. J. *The Story of Bing Crosby.* Cleveland, World
Publishing Co., 1946.
ULANOV, B. *The incredible Crosby.* New York, McGraw Hill,
1948.

Miles Davis (trumpeter)
JAMES, M. *Miles Davis.* London, Cassell, 1961. (Kings of jazz
series no. 9.) Brief biography with much critical material on
Davis' work.
—— —— New York, Barnes, 1961.

Sammy Davis Jr. (singer)
DAVIS, S., BOYAR, J. *and* BOYAR, J. *Yes I can: the story of
Sammy Davis Jr.* New York, Farrar, Straus and Giroux, 1965.
Biography of the Negro singer who has had jazz connections
throughout his career. A good example of a fringe artist (see
also Lena Horne, Hoagy Carmichael, etc.).
—— —— London, Cassell, 1965.

Johnny Dodds (clarinettist)
LAMBERT, G. E. *Johnny Dodds.* London, Cassell, 1961. (Kings
of jazz series no. 10.) Biography of a leading New Orleans
clarinet player who played with some of Louis Armstrong's
most important recorded groups.

Warren 'Baby' Dodds (drummer)
DODDS, W. *and* GARA, L. *The Baby Dodds story.* Los Angeles,
Contemporary Press, 1959. Life story of leading New Orleans
jazz drummer.

Duke Ellington (composer, bandleader and pianist)
See also the bio-discographies in Chapter 5.
GAMMOND, P. *ed. Duke Ellington: his life and music.* London,
Phoenix House, 1958. Essay collection.
—— —— New York, Roy Publishers, 1958.
—— —— London, Jazz Book Club, 1960.
LAMBERT, G. E. *Duke Ellington.* London, Cassell, 1959. (Kings
of jazz series no. 1.) Well-written but with little original
material.
—— —— New York, Barnes, 1961.

ULANOV, B. *Duke Ellington.* New York, Creative Age Press, 1946. Includes discography.
—— —— Buenos Aires, Editorial Estuardo, 1946. (In Spanish.)
—— —— London, Musicians Press, 1947.

J. B. 'Dizzy' Gillespie (trumpeter)
JAMES, M. *Dizzy Gillespie.* London, Cassell, 1959. (Kings of jazz series no. 2.) Rather dull evaluation of a colourful musician who was one of the leading influences in developing the 'modern' school of jazz.
—— —— New York, Barnes, 1961.

Benny Goodman (clarinettist and bandleader)
See also bio-discography in Chapter 5.
GOODMAN, B. *and* KOLODIN, I. *The kingdom of swing.* New York, Stackpole, 1939. Life of the leading musician of the big band swing era up to 1939.
—— —— New York, Ungar, 1961.
—— —— London, Constable, 1962. (Paperback edition.)

W. C. Handy (composer)
HANDY, W. C. *Father of the blues: an autobiography,* edited by Arna Bontemps. New York, Macmillan, 1941.
—— —— London, Sidgwick and Jackson, 1957.

Coleman Hawkins (tenor saxophonist)
McCARTHY, A. J. *Coleman Hawkins.* London Cassell, 1963. (Kings of jazz series no. 12.) Life of the most important single figure in the development of the saxophone in jazz whose work spans several periods and styles.

Ted Heath (trombonist and bandleader)
HEATH, T. *Listen to my music: an autobiography.* London, Muller, 1957. Life of the British orchestra leader whose band included many of the leading British jazz musicians in the 1940's and 1950's.

Billie Holiday (singer)
HOLIDAY, B. *and* DUFFTY, W. *Lady sings the blues.* Garden City, N.Y. Doubleday, 1956. Important because its subject is unique in jazz history, and not because of the way it is written. Includes discography.
—— —— London, Barrie and Rockliff, 1958.

Lena Horne (singer)
HORNE, L. *In person, Lena Horne: as told to Helen Arstein and Carlton Moss.* New York, Greenberg, 1950.
HORNE, L. *and* SCHICKEL, R. *Lena.* New York, Doubleday, 1965. Lena Horne is an important artiste in the 'jazz-popular music' fringe area.
—— —— London, Deutsch, 1966.

P. C. 'Spike' Hughes (bassist and composer)
HUGHES, P. C. *Second movement: continuing the autobiography of Spike Hughes.* London, Museum Press, 1951. Hughes was a composer and bass-player who was influential in the British jazz world in the early 1930's.

Pete Johnson (pianist)
MAURERER, H. J. *ed. The Pete Johnson story.* New York, The author, 1965. Life of leading boogie-woogie pianist.

Max Kaminsky (trumpeter)
KAMINSKY, M. *and* HUGHES, W. E. *My life in jazz.* New York, Harper and Row, 1963. Life and work of the Chicago-style trumpet player.
—— —— London, Deutsch, 1964.
—— —— London, Jazz Book Club, 1965.

George Lewis (clarinettist and bandleader)
STUART, J. A. *pseud* (i.e. Dorothy Tait). *Call him George.* London, Peter Davies, 1961. Life of George Lewis, New Orleans clarinet player.
—— —— London, Jazz Book Club, 1963.

Humphrey Lyttelton (trumpter and bandleader)
LYTTELTON, H. *I play as I please: the memoirs of an Old Etonian trumpeter.* London, MacGibbon and Kee, 1954. Biography covering the early years of Lyttelton's career in jazz. Amusing and interesting comments on the British jazz scene from 1945 to 1954.
—— —— London, Jazz Book Club, 1957.
—— —— London, Pan Books, 1959. (Paperback edition.)
—— *Second chorus.* London, MacGibbon and Kee, 1958. Further comments and reminiscences on British jazz between 1954 and 1958.
—— —— London, Jazz Book Club, 1960.

'Wingy' Manone (trumpeter)
MANONE, W. *and* VANDERVOORT, P. *Trumpet on the wing.*
New York, Doubleday, 1948. Life story of a traditional style
trumpeter.
—— —— London, Jazz Book Club, 1964.

George Melly (singer)
MELLY, G. *Owning-up.* London, Weidenfeld and Nicolson, 1965.
Earthy pen picture of life with a travelling jazz band (Mick
Mulligan) in Britain. Describes and removes most of the
glamour from the 'one-night-stand' existence of itinerant
bands.

Milton 'Mezz' Mezzrow (clarinettist and bandleader)
MEZZROW, M. *and* WOLFE, B. *Really the blues.* New York and
Toronto, Random House, 1946. Important biographical work
on Milton Mezzrow, a clarinet player, who played with many
leading jazz musicians and made some memorable gramo-
phone records.
—— —— London, Musicians Press, 1947.
—— —— London, Secker & Warburg, 1957. 'New edition.'
—— —— London, Transworld Publishers, 1961. (Paperback
edition.)

Ferdinand 'Jelly Roll' Morton (pianist, composer and bandleader)
LOMAX, A. *Mister Jelly Roll: the fortunes of Jelly Roll Morton,
New Orleans creole and 'inventor of jazz'.* New York, Duell,
1950. Vital and important work on the leading New Orleans
jazz pianist, composer and bandleader.
—— —— London, Cassell, 1952.
—— —— New York, Grove Press, 1956. (Paperback edition.)
—— —— London, Jazz Book Club, 1956.
—— —— London, Pan Books, 1959. (Paperback edition.)
WILLIAMS, M. T. *Jellyroll Morton.* London, Cassell, 1962. (Kings
of jazz series no. 11.)

Loring 'Red' Nichols (cornetist and bandleader)
JOHNSON, G. *The five pennies: the biography of jazz band leader
Red Nichols.* New York, Dell, 1959. Based on the film of the
same title (see also Chapter 8).

Joseph 'King' Oliver (cornetist and bandleader)
See also bio-discography in Chapter 5.

WILLIAMS, M. T. *King Oliver*. London, Cassell, 1960. (Kings of jazz series no. 8.) Brief life of a major jazz figure of the 1920's. Oliver led one of the most exciting and creative bands in jazz at this period.

Charlie Parker (alto saxophonist)
HARRISON, M. *Charlie Parker*. London, Cassell, 1960. (Kings of jazz series no.6). Major creative jazz musician whose influence has been enormous in the years since 1945. Parker was a pioneering figure in the cool sound of modern jazz.
———— ——— New York, Barnes, 1961.
REISNER, R. G. *Bird: the legend of Charlie Parker*. New York, Citadel Press, 1962. A collection of facts and legends about Parker, the saxophonist.
———— ——— London, MacGibbon and Kee, 1963.
———— ——— London, Jazz Book Club, 1965.

Django Reinhardt (guitarist)
DELAUNAY, C. *Django Reinhardt, souvenirs. Precedes d'un inedit de Jean Cocteau*. Paris, Editions Jazz-Hot, 1954. (In French.) Life of the French guitarist which includes a 78-page discography.
——— *Django Reinhardt*. Translated by Michael James. London, Cassell, 1961.
———— ——— London, Jazz Book Club, 1963.

Artie Shaw (clarinettist and bandleader)
SHAW, A. *The trouble with Cinderella: an outline of identity*. New York, Farrar, Straus and Young, 1952. Autobiography of a leading clarinet player and bandleader of the 'swing era' in the 1930's and 1940's.
———— ——— London, Jarrolds, 1955.
———— ——— New York, Collier Books, 1963. (Paperback ed.)

Bessie Smith (blues singer)
OLIVER, P. *Bessie Smith*. London, Cassell, 1959. (Kings of jazz series no. 3.) Fascinating story of a great artist. Bessie Smith's dramatic rise to fame and extremely tragic death are covered.
———— ——— New York, Barnes, 1961.

Willie 'The Lion' Smith (pianist)
SMITH, W. *and* HOEFFER, G. *Music on my mind: the memoirs of an American pianist*. New York, Doubleday, 1964.

—— —— London, MacGibbon and Kee, 1965.
—— —— London, Jazz Book Club, 1966.

Jack Teagarden (trombonist)
See also bio-discography in Chapter 5.
SMITH, J. D. *and* GUTTRIDGE, L. *Jack Teagarden : the story of a jazz maverick.* London, Cassell, 1960. A superficial book which is unworthy of the work of Teagarden, the trombone player from Texas who has played with Armstrong and many other leading musicians.
—— —— London, Jazz Book Club, 1962.

Thomas 'Fats' Waller (pianist, composer and bandleader)
See also bio-discographies in Chapter 5.
FOX, C. *Fats Waller.* London, Cassell, 1960. (Kings of jazz series no. 7.) Life of the pianist and composer, Thomas 'Fats' Waller.
—— —— New York, Barnes, 1961.
KIRKEBY, W. T. E. *and others. Ain't misbehavin' : the story of Fats Waller.* London, Peter Davies, 1966.
—— —— New York, Dodd, Mead, 1966.

Ethel Waters (singer)
WATERS, E. *and* SAMUELS, C. *His eye is on the sparrow : an autobiography.* New York, Doubleday, 1951.
—— —— London, W. H. Allen, 1951.
—— —— London, Jazz Book Club, 1958.
—— —— New York, Bantam Books, 1959. (Paperback edition.)

Paul Whiteman (bandleader)
WHITEMAN, P. *and* McBRIDE, M. M. *Jazz.* New York, Sears, 1926. Orchestra leader Paul Whiteman's main contribution to jazz was in providing work for some leading exponents. His band played 'symphonic jazz' which had little, if any, relation to the real thing.

CHAPTER 4

ANALYSIS, THEORY AND CRITICISM

Many writers have made their contributions to the jazz literature by attempting to analyse the musical structure and form. Some of these have found this task was beyond their knowledge either because they lacked essential experience of that elusive factor 'the feeling of jazz' or because their understanding of musical theory was faulty. This 'feel of jazz' is exceedingly difficult to define; it is a pragmatic thing which a true jazzman knows instinctively. Add to this the fact that much of jazz is not written down and that even scored jazz contains nuances which are impossible to notate and vary from musician to musician. This means that to write intelligently and critically on this subject requires particular skill. One writer who has this is English musicologist Wilfred Mellers and his *Music in a new found land* is an outstanding work. The book is not confined to jazz alone but covers authoritatively all aspects of American music. A major section of 140 pages is devoted to jazz and in this the author shows his awareness of the place of this idiom in the mainstream of music. Out of 543 pages, 70 are devoted to a comprehensive discography and in total this important document is essential reading. Another good analysis by a primarily classical composer is *The anatomy of jazz* by Leroy Ostransky. In the words of the preface 'this book is an attempt, first, to present jazz in its proper perspective to those whose primary interest is in "serious" or classical music and to relate jazz theory to music theory in general. Second to introduce to those whose primary interest is in jazz to the problems of non-jazz composers and performers by relating jazz to the history of music in general. Finally (to try) to indicate to jazzmen what I believe to be their present position in music as well as their musical responsibility to the future.' Dr. Ostransky's book is well documented and includes a comprehensive bibliography of books and periodicals on jazz. The first part of the book is perhaps the most valuable since the information given in the later chapters on jazz styles and periods can be found elsewhere. An interesting and controversial case is made in Henry Pleasants' *Death of a music.* This is a penetrating analysis of modern classical music and jazz; the controversial issue is indicated by the book's sub-title 'the decline of the European tradition and the rise of jazz'. The arguments advanced were continued and concluded in a further work by Pleasants titled *Serious music—and all that jazz* (1969). In this group of writers the final mention goes to Sidney Finkelstein whose *Jazz: a people's music* (1948) was a good analysis with the same general subject as the above quoted works. Finkelstein discusses improvisation and form quoting examples of the work of major Negro musicians. A political (Marxist?) flavour pervades this book which makes it unusual in the jazz literature.

It should be mentioned also that jazz has become an acceptable subject for university dissertations, although the end-products of these researches are often extremely difficult to gain access to. Examples are Hugh L. Smith's *Literary manifestation of a liberal romanticism in American jazz* which was accepted for a Ph.D. at the University of New Mexico in 1955 and Lois Von Haupt's *Jazz: an historical and analytical study* (New York University M.A. Thesis 1945).

The above works may be regarded as the product of knowledgeable, but uncommitted students of jazz; we can now consider the critical works of the jazz-based writer. Typical of these writers who understand the 'feeling of jazz' but are not necessarily expert musicians is the German author Joachim Berendt. Berendt's *New jazz book* is probably one of jazz literature's best sellers since it sold over 200,000 copies in the German edition issued in 1959 before appearing in English in 1964. It is a successful over-all view of the jazz field and its author seems to be free of the prejudices of some other leading jazz critics. The pattern followed by the book is to look at the various styles (arranged chronologically by decade), the major musicians and the various instruments used in playing jazz. Berendt has a chapter towards the end of the book in which he attempts that most difficult of tasks—to define exactly what jazz is. As one might expect from a German writer, the book is painstaking and methodical and is so presented as to be of value to the beginner in jazz or the expert.

Other major contributors from Continental Europe to this area of the literature are the French critics Hugues Panassie and Andre Hodeir. Much of Panassie's enthusiastic work may be read rather for the spirit than the letter and two particular books of his which have been translated into English are worthy of mention; *Hot jazz* which appeared in 1936 and *The real jazz*, 2nd ed. 1960. The former title is in fact a major landmark in jazz criticism. These two books can be considered together since they are closely connected. The treatment of the subject in each follows a certain pattern: first an explanation of what Panassie feels jazz is, followed by chapters devoted to musicians grouped by the instrument they play, e.g. the trumpet, the trombone, etc. Comparison of the two books is interesting, particularly in considering Panassie's assessments of the same musician at different periods of his life. He wrote the first book under the severe handicap of not having heard many of the really influential players and the later book attempts to correct many of his admitted errors of judgement. Panassie has no time for modern jazz styles and contends that these styles do not belong to jazz itself. A great protagonist of the American Negro, he was most reluctant to admit that Whites could play 'real' jazz.

Andre Hodeir's work is a complete contrast to the work of his fellow-countryman. Some critics feel he is the leading writer on jazz in the French language and his major contribution is probably *Jazz: its evolution and essence* which appeared in English in 1956. It was originally published in 1954 under the title *Hommes et problèmes du jazz.* This book is a complex, intellectual appraisal of jazz which is not particularly easy to read for the musically uneducated. Hodeir has produced a first-class study with a bias towards the modern schools of jazz. There is a good chapter on the influence of jazz on European music and a discography of records cited in the text. In spite of some confusion over the relative importance of taste and technical skill in connection with early jazz, this is one of the select few major works of jazz criticism. *Toward jazz* by the same author is a collection of essays written between 1953 and 1959 for a variety of journals and anthologies. Two other books by Hodeir written in the 1940's appeared only in French. These are *Le jazz c'est inconnu* (1945) and *Introduction à la musique de jazz* (1948).

Leonard Feather is justly renowned for his compilation of major works of reference in the jazz field and these are fully discussed in the next chapter. He has also contributed to the critical literature and *Inside jazz* (which appeared in 1949 with its original title *Inside be-bop*) was a combination of technical analysis and history covering the period 1940–1949. *The book of jazz: a guide to the entire field* is authoritative and presents its information in a rather unusual (but very useful) way. There are the four main sections, on (*a*) the sources, (*b*) the instruments, sounds and performers, (*c*) the nature of jazz, and (*d*) the future of jazz. Another important American book is Winthrop Sargeant's *Jazz: a history.* This is a misleading title since it is not by any means a history of jazz, but rather an essay in comparative musicology; its approach also is somewhat unusual. It has many musical examples within its pages and analyses jazz as a distinct musical idiom. It traces its origins, dissects its anatomy and describes in detail those features which distinguish it from other varieties of music. It has a useful bibliography of some 150 items all published before 1940 and is required reading for any serious jazz student. Another almost classic work is Wilder Hobson's *American jazz music.* This was written at the height of the 'swing' era in jazz history and before the birth of modern jazz. It is an intelligent and perceptive assessment of jazz up to 1940. British journalist Iain Lang's *Jazz in perspective* (1947) is a useful book. The 40-page chapter on 'The blues' is particularly good but the book went out-of-print somewhat prematurely. It reappeared in a book club edition in 1957 and was also translated into Italian. Other British contributions of some interest are the four annual volumes edited by Messrs. Traill and Lascelles in the *Just Jazz* series. These appeared from 1957 to 1960 and contained essays of a varying standard on a wide variety of topics. Approximately 50 per cent of each volume is given to a complete jazz discography for the year. This latter function is now continued by the annual publication *Jazz catalogue* which is discussed further in the next chapter. Ex-jazz musician Benny Green's book *The reluctant art* is perceptive and informative. It takes the form of five critical essays on the work of Goodman, Holiday, Beiderbecke, Young and Parker, all of whom are regarded by the author as major influences in jazz history. Green succeeds in writing entertainingly and in sorting out legend from fact in several cases.

Turning to the American critics, we find a number of works in the form of collected essays, some of which appeared originally in jazz journals. Typical is Ralph de Toledano's *Frontiers of Jazz* which first appeared in 1947. This collection is divided into two sections: section one is entitled 'The anatomy of jazz' and consists of five contributions (including a brief one by Jean Paul Sartre) while section two on 'the men who made jazz' covers a wide range of earlier jazz musicians from King Oliver through the New Orleans Rhythm Kings to Benny Goodman and Duke Ellington. Grossman and Farrell's *Heart of jazz* has a scholarly approach to its limited area of interest. It is strongly biased towards traditional jazz—in particular the work of West Coast musicians of the 1940's and is a well intentioned but misguided special pleading for recognition of the work of Lu Watters and his colleagues. Shapiro and Hentoff's *Jazzmakers* (1957) (referred to in Chapter 3) is an exceptional work and, as with all the other publications of these authors, worthy of study. Three other Americans, Barry Ulanov, John S. Wilson and Martin Williams, are all critics who have made significant contributions. Ulanov's *Handbook of jazz* appeared in 1957 and this period between then and 1963 was a period of prolific jazz writing. John Wilson's *Jazz: the transition years, 1940–1960* was published later than this period and in some ways it is comparable to Francis Newton's *Jazz scene* (see Chapter 1). Wilson is jazz critic of the *New York Times* and his well-produced book includes in the final two chapters a survey of the impact of jazz outside the United States and on mass audiences everywhere. *The art of jazz* and *Jazz panorama* are two essay collections edited by Martin Williams. The latter consists of essays collected from the pages of the short-lived American magazine *Jazz Review*, whilst the former is made up of items from various sources including sleeve notes from long-playing records. A particularly interesting piece in *The art of jazz* is the contribution from the conductor, Ernst Ansermet, on Will Marion Cook's Orchestra which toured Europe in 1918. Most of the contributors are well-known critics from both sides of the Atlantic and the general standard of writing is high. Further essay collections showing literary merit and interesting jazz content are Burnett James *Essays on jazz* (1961) and the three volumes by Whitney Balliett. The latter are reprinted items mainly from the *New Yorker* and are entitled *The sound of surprise* (1959), *Dinosaurs in the morning* (1962) and *Such sweet thunder* (1966). Balliett's work is outstanding. He is a critic of catholic taste whose comments are always highly intelligent and stimulating. The essays in these three volumes cover the period 1954–1966 and are of both a critical and biographical nature. British critic Benny Green has described him as 'the most literate of all jazz writers'.

A collection of essays originally published by leading American literary magazines are by Negro writer Ralph Ellison under the collective title *Shadow and act* (1967). About one-third of the book is devoted to jazz and there are outstanding pieces on Mahalia Jackson, Charlie Parker and Jimmy Rushing. Ellison is a fluent writer who is comparable to Le Roi Jones, Langston Hughes and James Baldwin for quality of work and deep interest in the Negro musical heritage. *The jazz word*, a collection of miscellaneous essays edited by Dom Cerulli and others, has a few good pieces but in the main displays the worst excesses of jazz writing.

Critics who have specialised in discussing the work of

modern jazzmen are Raymond Horricks, Alun Morgan, Barry McRae and A. B. Spellman (another Negro critic). 'Modern' jazz is, of course, the label applied to a school of playing developed since the mid-1940's following the pioneering of Charlie Parker and Dizzy Gillespie. The critical works by these authors, and by Michael James in *Ten modern jazzmen,* are invaluable to any reader wishing to understand this branch of jazz music. Included are various sub-groupings of cool music, 'avant-garde' and 'free-form' and McRae's *Jazz cataclysm* (1967) provides a concise and readable account of developments by such jazzmen as John Coltrane, Sonny Rollins and particularly Ornette Coleman. This book has a useful selected discography to complete each of the 12 chapters. Spellman confines his work to a critical assessment of four 'modernists' including Coleman in *Four lives in the be-bop business.* The other three musicians discussed are Cecil Taylor, Herbie Nichols and Jackie McLean. Horricks, Morgan and others combined to produce two books on this group of jazz musicians. Their books are *Modern jazz* (1956) and *These jazzmen of our time* (1959), both originally published in Britain by Gollancz.

Before leaving the books of criticism and analysis altogether, it will be appropriate to consider a small number of titles which have appeared in recent years as part of the literature for children. Some of these titles are very successful in explaining to younger readers what jazz is all about and play an important part in catching the interest of future generations of jazz connoisseurs. Typical products of the American publishing houses are Donald Myrus' *I like jazz* (1964) and Lillian Erlich's *What jazz is all about.* The latter book is also a useful introductory text for adults since Mrs. Erlich writes succinctly and accurately. She includes some good photographs (which are essential in this type of book) and there is a short selected bibliography of further reading. Another recent book which is more analytical than historical is Martin Williams' *Where's the melody* (1966). R. P. Jones' *Jazz* which appeared in the useful Methuen Outlines series in 1963 is compact and informative while *Enjoying jazz* by Rex Harris is a young person's guide to traditional jazz only. There is a useful seven-page guide to further reading which greatly adds to the value of this book.

Gammond and Clayton's *Know about jazz* is another excellent British contribution to the jazz primers and in its 62 pages gets down to basic essentials. The book is beautifully designed, well laid out typographically and contains a mixture of good photographs, line drawings and colourful paintings. The final 15 pages are devoted to brief biographies (listing selected records) of leading jazz artists and the end papers of the book contain a brief glossary of jazz terminology—altogether excellent value and very suitable for the market it is directed at.

Humorous writings on jazz are rare indeed but two examples can be mentioned. Leonard Feather and Jack Tracy produced *Laughter from the hip* in 1963 and in Britain *Fourteen miles on a clear night* (1966) by Peter Gammond and Peter Clayton was subtitled 'an irreverent, sceptical and affectionate book about jazz records'. This collection of brief anecdotes is not outstandingly good but then jazz is a serious subject, it seems!

Books on the playing, composing and arranging of jazz vary from the excellent to the utterly worthless. Mentioned here only because it might be the worst book ever written on the subject is Martin Lindsay's *Teach yourself jazz.* This was an extraordinary choice for such a normally excellent series. Better, but still generally unsatisfactory, is Sinclair Traill's *Play that music* which is a collection of brief essays each describing the approach to various instruments by well-known British practitioners. However, the difficulty of explaining by means of the printed word how to play jazz does excuse a book like *Play that music* to some extent. Much better are the books on composing and arranging and William Russo's *Composing for the jazz orchestra* is a brief but useful volume. It is particularly good for its elaborate description of chords, their nomenclature and voicings. Russo made his name composing and arranging for the Stan Kenton orchestra and his other contribution to the literature is *Jazz composition and orchestration* (1968). This is a vast book of 825 pages which includes hundreds

of examples and is of major importance in this field. Also
for the more experienced musician with good technical
skills, Jerry Coker's *Improvising jazz* is a useful, practical
manual. Coker does succeed in getting down on to paper
much of the elusive knowledge necessary to the modern-
style jazzman. In this particular field of interest his book is
thus very valuable.
Finally there are the specialised works dealing with
playing jazz on a particular instrument. There are a number
of manuals instructing the player of wind and brass instruments but the most important in this field have been
produced for the pianist. Duke Ellington produced his
Piano method for the blues as far back as 1943 which also
contained a history and analysis of the blues form. More
recently there is the important work of John Mehegan.
Mehegan's chief contribution is a four-volume work *Jazz
improvisation* issued in the 1960's. Volume one systematises and defines the fundamental musical concepts of the
art of jazz improvisation, while volume two discusses jazz
rhythm and the improvised line. This volume contains
transcriptions of 29 recorded solos by Louis Armstrong,
Roy Eldridge, Art Tatum, Charlie Parker and Stan Getz.
The third volume is entitled 'Swing and early progressive
piano styles' and closely analyses piano styles from the
period 1935–1950. This covers the work of such musicians
as Teddy Wilson, Art Tatum, Bud Powell and George
Shearing. The final volume in this important series deals
with contemporary piano styles and covers the period 1950
to 1965.

BIBLIOGRAPHY

BALLIETT, W. *Dinosaurs in the morning: 41 pieces on jazz.*
Philadelphia, Lippincott, 1962. Collection of essays originally
written for the *New Yorker* magazine.
——— London, Phoenix House, 1964.
——— London, Jazz Book Club, 1965.
——— *The sound of surprise: 46 pieces of jazz.* New York, Dutton,
1959. Collection of brief essays on all fields of jazz which
originally appeared in various American periodicals between
1954 and 1959.

—— —— London, Kimber, 1960.

—— —— London, Jazz Book Club, 1962.

—— —— London, Penguin Books, 1963. Paperback edition with discography.

—— *Such sweet thunder.* New York, Bobbs-Merrill, 1966. Continues the collected essays of previous volumes. All were written between 1962 and 1966 for the *New Yorker.*

—— —— London, Macdonald, 1968.

BERENDT, J. *Das neues Jazzbuch: Entwickling und Bedeutung der Jazzmusik.* Frankfurt, Fischer Bucherei, 1959 (in German). Overall view of jazz which is balanced in content and useful to both the beginner and the expert.

—— *The new jazz book: a history and guide.* Translated by Daniel Morgenstern. New York, Hill and Wang, 1962.

—— —— London, Peter Owen, 1964.

—— —— London, Jazz Book Club, 1965.

BORNEMAN, E. *A critic looks at jazz.* London, Jazz Music Books, 1946.

BRYCE, O. and McLAREN, A. *Lets play jazz: a beginner's guide to jazz.* Bushey, Herts., The Authors, 1965.

CERULLI, D. *and others. The jazz word.* New York, Ballantine Books, 1960. Literary excerpts.

—— —— London, Dobson, 1962.

—— —— London, Jazz Book Club, 1963.

COKER, J. *Improvising jazz.* Englewood Cliffs, N.J., Prentice-Hall, 1964. Useful manual for the modern jazzman.

CONDON, E. *and* GEHMAN, R. *Treasury of jazz.* New York, Dial Press, 1956.

—— —— London, Peter Davies, 1957.

DANCE, S. *ed. Jazz era: the Forties.* London, MacGibbon and Kee, 1961. Survey of the jazz records of the period 1940–1949. Covers the birth of modern jazz and the revival of traditional styles.

—— —— London, Jazz Book Club, 1962.

DANKWORTH, A. *Jazz: an introduction to its musical basis.* London, Oxford University Press, 1968. Brief 90-page book which deals sketchily with the musical 'guts' of jazz. Part 1 covers chords, forms, scales, rhythm and tonal effects while Part 2 deals with the development of jazz styles and instrumentation. The three appendices do not add significantly to the book's value and appendix C 'Books on jazz' only lists three titles.

DE TOLEDANO, R. *ed. Frontiers of jazz.* New York, Durrell, 1947.

Collection of essays written between 1926 and 1947, each with an introduction by the editor. They are selected from both jazz and non-jazz periodicals.

—— —— 2nd ed. New York, Ungar, 1962.

—— —— London, Jazz Book Club, 1966.

ELLINGTON, D. *Piano method for blues.* New York, Robbins Music Corporation, 1943. A history and analysis of the blues form.

ELLISON, R. *Shadow and act.* New York, Random House, 1964. Essay contributions to leading American literary magazines. About one-third of the collection is devoted to jazz.

—— —— London, Secker and Warburg, 1967.

ERLICH, L. *What jazz is all about, illustrated with a portrait gallery of jazz greats.* New York, Messner, 1962. Useful introductory text mainly aimed at young adults.

—— —— London, Gollancz, 1963.

ESQUIRE'S jazz book. Edited by Paul Eduard Miller, New York, Smith and Durrell, 1944. Annual publication containing selections from *Esquire* magazine.

ESQUIRE'S 1945 jazz book. New York, Barnes, 1945.

ESQUIRE'S 1946 jazz book. New York, Barnes, 1946.

ESQUIRE'S 1947 jazz book. Edited by E. Anderson. New York, Smith and Durrell, 1947. *See also* MILLER, P. E. *and* VENABLES, R. *eds.*

ESQUIRE'S world of jazz. Edited by L. W. Gillenson. Commentary by James Poling. New York, Grosset and Dunlap, 1962. Superb artistic publication particularly notable for the illustrations and modernistic paintings. Basically a collection of essays on jazz with a 12-page selective discography by John Lessner covering all styles.

—— —— London, A. Barker, 1963.

—— —— London, Jazz Book Club, 1964.

FEATHER, L. *The book of jazz: a guide to the entire field.* New York, Horizon Press, 1957. Authoritative work including particularly useful section analysing the role of the various instruments in jazz.

—— —— London, A. Barker, 1959.

—— —— New York, Meridian Books, 1960. Paperback ed.?

—— —— London, Jazz Book Club, 1961.

—— *The book of jazz from then till now: a guide to the entire field.* Rev. ed. New York, Horizon Press, 1965. Revised edition of *The book of jazz.*

—— *Inside jazz* (originally entitled *Inside bebop*). New York,

Robbins, 1949. History and technical analysis of jazz together with biographies of jazzmen. Covers the period 1940–1949.

FEATHER, L. *and* TRACY, J. *Laughter from the hip.* New York, Horizon Press, 1963. Jazz humour.

FINKELSTEIN, S. *Jazz: a people's music.* New York, Citadel Press, 1948. Good analytical text which attempts to fit jazz into its place in musical history.

—— —— London, Jazz Book Club, 1964.

GAMMOND, P. *and* CLAYTON, P. *Fourteen miles on a clear night: an irreverent, sceptical and affectionate book about jazz records.* London, Peter Owen, 1966. Collection of humorous anecdotes about jazz.

—— —— London, Jazz Book Club, 1967.

—— *Know about jazz.* London and Glasgow, Blackie, 1963. Introductory primer.

—— —— Toronto, Ryerson P., 1964.

GLEASON, R. J. *ed. Jam session: an anthology of jazz.* New York, Putnams, 1958. Essay collection with bibliography.

—— —— London, Peter Davies, 1958.

—— —— London, Jazz Book Club, 1961.

GREEN, B. *The reluctant art: five studies in the growth of jazz.* London, MacGibbon and Kee, 1962. Essays on the work of Benny Goodman, Billie Holiday, Bix Beiderbecke, Lester Young and Charlie Parker.

—— —— New York, Horizon Press, 1963.

—— —— London, Jazz Book Club, 1964.

GROSSMAN, W. L. *and* FARRELL, J. W. *The heart of jazz.* New York, New York University Press, 1956. Scholarly approach to the work of West Coast 'revivalist' jazz musicians.

—— —— London, Vision Press, 1958.

HARRIS, R. *Enjoying jazz.* London, Phoenix House, 1960. Young person's guide to traditional jazz, with bibliography.

—— —— New York, Roy, 1960.

—— —— London, Jazz Book Club, 1961.

—— —— revised ed. London, Phoenix House, 1963.

HEATON, P. *Jazz.* London, Burke, 1964. A primer of jazz mainly suitable for the newcomer to the subject.

—— —— Toronto, Ambassador Press, 1964.

HOBSON, W. *American jazz music.* New York, Norton, 1939. Important work on pre-1939 jazz music.

—— —— London, Dent, 1941.

—— —— London, Jazz Book Club, 1956.

HODEIR, A. *Introduction à la musique de jazz.* Paris, Larousse, 1948. (In French.)
—— *Le jazz c'est inconnu.* Paris, Editions France-Empire, 1945. (In French.)
—— *Toward jazz.* Translated by Noel Burch. New York, Grove Press, 1962. Essay collection written between 1953 and 1959.
—— —— London, Jazz Book Club, 1965.
—— *Hommes et problemes du jazz; suivi de la religion du jazz.* Paris, Portulan, 1954. (In French.) Important intellectual appraisal suitable for the musically educated, but marred by the author's misunderstanding of the nature of the earliest kinds of jazz.
—— *Jazz: its evolution and essence.* Translated by David Noakes from 'Hommes et problèmes du jazz'. New York, Grove Press, 1956.
—— —— London, Secker and Warburg, 1956.
—— —— London, Jazz Book Club, 1958.
JAMES, B. *Essays on jazz.* London, Sidgwick and Jackson, 1961.
—— —— London, Jazz Book Club, 196?.
—— —— *Living forwards.* London, Cassell, 1961. Biography of a leading British musical critic who writes on jazz.
JAZZWAYS: a yearbook of hot music. Edited by G. S. Rosenthal. Cincinnati, Jazzways, 1946.
—— —— London, Musicians Press, 1947.
JONES, M. *and* McCARTHY, A. J. *eds. Jazz review: a miscellany.* London, Jazz Music Books, 1945. A selection of notes and essays on live and recorded jazz, most of which were wiitten in the U.S.A. before the end of the war.
JONES, R. P. *Jazz.* London, Methuen, 1963. (Methuen's outlines series.) For children.
—— —— New York, Roy Publications, 1963.
LANG, I. *Background of the blues.* London, Workers Music Association, 1943. Brief volume which was expanded in 1947 into *Jazz in perspective.* 'An expansion of an essay written for the first volume of Leonard Russell's *Saturday book*'—foreword.
—— *Jazz in perspective: the background of the blues.* London and New York, Hutchinson, 1947. Influential book particularly in Britain. Good on the blues. Published in Italian under the title of *Il Jazz* translated by Roberto Leydi.
—— —— London, Jazz Book Club, 1957.
LARKIN, P. *All what jazz: a record diary, 1961–68.* London, Faber, 1970. Collection of articles from the *Daily Telegraph.*

LATEEF, Y. *Yusef Lateef's flute book of the blues.* Teaneck, N.J., Almur Music, 1965.

LINDSAY, M. *Teach yourself jazz.* London, English Universities Press, 1958. Little value as a manual of jazz.

LONGSTREET, S. *The real jazz, old and new.* Baton Rouge, Louisiana State University Press, 1956. Very personal account (illustrated by the author) of the traditional styles of jazz. Plenty of errors of fact included.

McCARTHY, A. J. *The trumpet in jazz.* London, Citizen Press, 1945.

—— ed. *Jazzbook 1947.* London, Editions Poetry, 1947. (Cover title: *PL Jazzbook 1947.*)

—— ed. *Jazzbook 1955.* London, Cassell, 1955.

—— ed. *The PL yearbook of jazz.* London, Editions Poetry, 1946. Essay collections.

McCARTHY, A. J. and JONES, M. eds. *Piano jazz.* London, Jazz Music Books, 1945. Biographical sketches of jazz pianists.

McRAE, B. *The jazz cataclysm.* London, Dent, 1967. Covers modern jazz and is particularly good on Ornette Coleman and his 'free-form' style. There is a selected discography with each of the twelve chapters.

—— —— New York, Barnes, 1967.

MATTHEW, B. *Trad mad.* London, World Distributors, 1962. Paperback edition. Ephemeral work on the traditional jazz boom of the early 1960's in Britain.

MEHEGAN, J. *Jazz improvisation.* 4 volumes. New York, Watson-Guptill. Volume 1: *Tonal and rhythmic principles,* 1958. Systematises and defines the fundamental musical concepts of the art of jazz improvisation. Volume 2: *Jazz rhythm and the improvised line,* 1962. Contains transcriptions of 29 recorded solos by Louis Armstrong, Roy Eldridge, Art Tatum, Charlie Parker, Stan Getz and others. Volume 3: *Swing and early progressive piano styles.* Piano styles from the period 1935–1960 are closely analysed. Covers the work of Teddy Wilson, Art Tatum, Bud Powell, George Shearing, etc. Volume 4: *Contemporary piano styles,* 1965. Covers the period 1950 to 1965 and uses the work of Oscar Peterson and others as examples.

—— —— New York, Simon & Schuster, 1968. (Paperback edition.)

—— *The jazz pianist.* New York, Watson-Guptill, 19?.

MELLERS, W. *Music in a new found land: themes and development in the history of American music.* London, Barrie and

Rockliff, 1964. Required reading for all jazz students. Pages 262–391 are devoted to jazz.
—— —— New York, Knopf, 1965.
MILLER, P. E. *and* VENABLES, R. *eds. Jazz book: from the Esquire jazz books 1944–1946.* London, Peter Davies, 1947.
MILLER, W. R. *The world of pop music and jazz.* St. Louis, Mo., Concordia, 1965.
MORGAN, A. *and* HORRICKS, R. *Modern jazz: a survey of developments since 1939.* London, Gollancz, 1956.
MYRUS, D. *Ballads, blues and the big beat.* New York, Macmillan, 1966.
—— *I like jazz.* New York, Collier-Macmillan, 1964. Ephemeral and anecdotal (all the well known ones!) and of no permanent value. Useful as an introductory text for children.
OSTRANSKY, L. *The anatomy of jazz.* Seattle, University of Washington Press, 1960. Well documented analytical text which includes a comprehensive and international bibliography of books and periodicals on jazz.
PANASSIE, H. *La bataille du jazz.* Paris, Editions Albin Michel, 1965. (In French.)
—— *Histoires des disques swing enregistres à New-York par Tommy Ladnier, Mezz Mezzrow, Frank Newton, etc.* Geneva, Grasset, 1944. (In French.)
—— *Le jazz hot.* Paris, Correa, 1934. (In French.) The French critic's first important work which has been a major influence in jazz criticism.
—— *Hot jazz: the guide to swing music.* Translated by Lyle and Eleanor Dowling from *Le jazz hot.* London, Cassell, 1936.
—— —— New York, Witmark, 1936.
—— *Jazz panorama.* Paris, Deux Rives, 1950. (In French.)
—— *La musique de jazz et le swing.* Paris, Correa, 1945. (In French.)
—— *La véritable musique de jazz.* Paris, Laffont, 1946. (In French.)
—— —— Ed. rev. et augm. Paris, Laffont, 1952.
—— *The real jazz.* New York, Smith and Durrell, 1942. Much more accurate assessment than in *Hot jazz.*
—— *The real jazz.* 2nd ed. revised and enlarged. Translated by Anne S. Williams. New York, Barnes, 1960.
—— —— London, Yoseloff, 1960.
—— London, Jazz Book Club, 1967.
PAUL, E. *That crazy American music.* Indianapolis, Bobbs-Merrill, 1957. Ephemeral and somewhat misleading account of jazz.

—— *That crazy music: the story of North American jazz*. London, Muller, 1957.

PLEASANTS, H. *Death of a music? the decline of the European tradition and the rise of jazz*. London, Gollancz, 1961. Penetrating analysis of modern classical music and jazz.

—— —— London, Jazz Book Club, 1962.

—— *Serious music—and all that jazz: an adventure in musical criticism*. London, Gollancz, 1969.

RUSSO, W. *Composing for the jazz orchestra*. Chicago and London, Chicago University Press, 1961. Brief 90-page volume which is chiefly useful for its elaborate description of chords, their nomenclature and voicings.

—— *Jazz composition and orchestration*. Chicago, Chicago University Press, 1968. A massive 825-page textbook for the would-be jazz arranger and composer. Is a scholarly musical analysis of harmony, counterpoint, voicing and form.

SARGEANT, W. *Jazz: hot and hybrid*. New York, Arrow, 1938. Valuable book which is required reading for the keen enthusiast.

—— —— New and enlarged ed. New York, Dutton, 1946.

—— *Jazz: a history*. Revised ed. New York, McGraw Hill, 1964.

SIMON, G. T. *The feeling of jazz*. New York, Simon and Schuster, 1961.

SMITH, H. L. *The literary manifestation of a liberal romanticism in American jazz*. Albuquerque, University of New Mexico, 1955. (Unpublished doctoral dissertation.)

SPELLMAN, A. B. *Four lives in the bebop business*. New York, Pantheon Books, 1966. Discusses the work of four modern jazz musicians—Cecil Taylor, Ornette Coleman, Herbie Nicholls and Jackie McLean.

—— —— London, MacGibbon and Kee, 1967.

TRAILL, S. *ed. Concerning jazz*. London, Faber, 1957. Collection of essays on various topics mainly by British critics.

—— —— London, Jazz Book Club, 1958.

—— *Play that music: a guide to playing jazz*. London, Faber, 1956. Contributions by leading British jazz musicians.

—— —— London, Jazz Book Club, 1958.

TRAILL, S. *and* LASCELLES, G. *eds. Just jazz*. 4 volumes. Volume 1: London, Peter Davies, 1957. Volume 2: London, Peter Davies, 1958. Volume 3: London, Landsborough Publications, 1959. Volume 4: London, Souvenir Press, 1960. Essay collections and comprehensive discographies of each year.

—— —— Volume 4: London, Jazz Book Club, 1961.
ULANOV, B. *A handbook of jazz.* New York, Viking Press, 1957.
—— —— London, Hutchinson, 1958.
VON HAUPT, L. *Jazz: an historical and analytical study.* New York, New York University Graduate School, 1945. (Unpublished M.A. thesis.)
WILLIAMS, M. T. *ed. The art of jazz: essays on the nature and development of jazz.* New York, Oxford University Press, 1959. Twenty-one essays on all aspects of jazz originally published as journal articles or as sleeve notes to long playing records. Each item is introduced by the editor giving the source and date of the original publication and there are brief discographies attached to each essay.
—— —— New York, Grove Press, 1960. (Paperback edition?)
—— —— London, Cassell, 1960.
—— —— London, Jazz Book Club, 1962.
—— *Jazz panorama: from the pages of* Jazz Review. New York, Crowell-Collier, 1962. Thirty-nine carefully selected pieces which together add up to a necessary book for anyone with more than a routine interest in jazz. Spoiled by the lack of an index.
—— —— New York, Crowell, 1964. Paperback ed.
—— —— London, Jazz Book Club, 1965.
—— *Where's the melody?: a listener's introduction to jazz.* New York, Pantheon Books, 1966. Analytical primer of jazz.
—— —— New York, Minerva Books, 1967. (Paperback edition.)
WILLIAMSON, K. *ed. This is jazz.* London, Newnes, 1960. Essay collection including contributions on Basie, Teagarden, Miles Davis, Broonzy, Ellington, Ella Fitzgerald, Billie Holiday, Sarah Vaughan, Morton. Translated into German in 1964.
—— —— London, Jazz Book Club, 1961.
WILSON, C. *Brandy of the damned: discourses of a musical eclectic.* London, John Baker, 1964.
—— *Chords and discords: purely personal opinions on music.* New York, Crown Publishers, 1966. (American ed. of *Brandy of the damned.*)
WILSON, J. S. *Jazz: the transition years, 1940–1960.* New York, Appleton-Century-Crofts, 1966. Well produced and useful book. Last two chapters particularly valuable as they survey the impact of jazz in the world outside the U.S.A. and on mass audiences. Glossary, discography and reading list are included.

CHAPTER 5

REFERENCE SOURCES

The treatment of jazz in the general reference sources available varies very widely. The standard work on music is Grove's *Dictionary of music and musicians* and in the 5th edition in 1954, the article on jazz, which occupied 6 pages, was written by the French critic Hugues Panassie. This was a reasonably good survey of the traditional and mainstream styles of jazz but Panassie, as usual, ignored the existence of the modern field. The bibliography of books and periodicals includes 11 books of Panassie's own; rather an unbalanced selection one feels. Many of the periodicals listed are only of marginal interest. Percy Scholes' article in the *Oxford companion to music* is completely inaccurate and is written in a patronising and denigrating manner. It is a completely worthless resumé and disgraces a standard work of such general excellence. The ideas of the author are quite obviously based on a single book—Osgood's *So this is jazz* (see Chapter 2) which was written in the mid 1920's. *Chambers' Encyclopaedia,* the major English work, gives 2 pages in Volume 8 to jazz music. In the 1959 edition the article was written by the Hungarian composer Matyas Seiber who tries to present a brief musical analysis of jazz, but the complete article is unsatisfactory and unworthy of a reference work such as Chambers. There is no mention of either the major figures in jazz, of the varying and complex styles, or of the tremendous influence of jazz throughout the world. The addition of Charles Fox as collaborator for the 1966 edition brought about a much-needed improvement to the article and many of the faults were cured. A further useful feature in this edition is the brief bibliography of four important jazz books. The *Encyclopedia Britannica* 1966 edition devotes 3 pages to jazz music, written by American jazz critic Martin T. Williams. This is an intelligent essay on the subject and is the best of the articles in the four standard general reference works quoted.

Specialised reference books dealing only with jazz are dominated by the works of Leonard Feather. Feather's work is widely acclaimed, and rightly so, since he covers the entire field from Texas blues singers to avante-garde pianists. The formula adopted by the author in *The encyclopedia of jazz* leaves the main section to cover biographical details of musicians, arrangers, critics, composers, etc. Each entry gives basic details such as instruments played, date and place of birth, brief career details, main recordings and address. Supplementary to this section are general articles on various aspects of jazz, plus discographies, a bibliography, a list of organisations and a list of record companies. Lists of magazine poll winners and 'blindfold' test comments are the least useful features. The first edition of Feather appeared in 1955 and was supplemented in 1956 by an *Encyclopedia yearbook of jazz.* A complete revision of the main work appeared in 1961 and had over 150 pages more than its predecessor. In 1966 *The encyclopedia of jazz in the Sixties* was published and is, in fact, virtually a third edition. It contains over 1,100 biographies and 200 photographs and musicians of all styles are included with the accent being placed on their recent work of importance.

More specialised still is Samuel Charters' *Jazz: New Orleans, 1885–1963* which is an index to the Negro musicians of New Orleans. This originally appeared in 1958 and was issued in a revised edition by a different publisher in 1963. The book is divided by periods with sections on 1885–1899; 1899–1919; 1919–1931 and 1931 to date. Each of these sections is further divided into biographies of musicians (in the case of section one this is further divided into the Downtown musicians and the Uptown musicians) and details of the major brass bands and orchestras. In the 2nd edition there is also some supplementary material in addenda at the end of each section. Appendices on discographical and source material are also included and there are indexes to names of musicians, names of bands, names of halls, cabarets, theatres etc. in New Orleans, tune titles and cities and towns in the delta region of Louisiana. Further encyclopedic coverage of the New Orleans jazz scene is in *New Orleans jazz: a family album* (1967). This valuable guide to the jazz musicians of New Orleans is written by Al Rose and Edmond Souchon. It includes over a thousand biographical sketches as well as comprehensive lists of jazz and brass bands belonging to the city. There is a unique collection of over 500 photographs, many of which were previously unpublished. Another work of importance, which complements rather than overlaps the above titles, is the *Dictionary of jazz* by Hugues Panassie and Madeleine Gautier. This was originally published in French in 1954, two years before the English translation appeared. The title of the American edition is *Guide to jazz.* It contains the usual Panassie prejudices and one critic described it as 'a collection of opinions, peppered with facts. . . .' Nevertheless, within its limitations it is good value and useful.

Other encyclopedic approaches to the subject have been made by French, German, Italian and Danish writers. Jorgensen and Wiedemann's *Mosaik jazz-lexicon* is a 400-page volume with over 1,700 headings giving information on the lives of important musicians. As might be expected, this work is particularly strong on the Scandinavian artists. Preceding the lexicon section is a short history of jazz which considers the social background as an important factor. There is also a comprehensive bibliography. The book has appeared up to now in both Danish and German editions. A work which has appeared in German and French is *Knaur's jazz lexicon* by Dauer and Longstreet. The original version appeared in 1957 and the French translation in 1959. A very recent French work is Tenot and Carl's *Dictionnaire du jazz* (1967) and a massive *Enciclopedia del jazz* by Gian Carlo Testoni and others was published in Italian in 1953.

More sociological than musical is Robert Gold's *Jazz lexicon* which is sub-titled 'An A–Z dictionary of jazz terms in the vivid idiom of America's most successful nonconformist minority'. It is a comprehensive and readable listing of jazz slang and terminology. Each word is defined and traced back to its earliest recorded use. Its semantic development is given and a note of its currency or degree of obsolescence is included. The book is the product of scholarly research by the author, who is Associate Professor of English at Jersey City State College, and is of interest both to the student of jazz and the student of linguistics.

There is also a small group of books which consist mainly of jazz photographs. Of these Dennis Stock's *Jazz street* (1960), which has a 63-page introduction by Nat Hentoff, is perhaps the best. The 130 photographs selected are unusual and interesting; they show jazzmen of all schools at work and at leisure. An early collection which appeared originally in 1939 and was re-issued in 1964 was *Swing photo album* by Timme Rosenkrantz and also worthy of mention is John Oliver's *Jazz classic* which appeared in 1962.

Jazz discography is an esoteric sub-culture with experts of its own and Paul Sheatsley, in a 1964 article in *Record Research*, covers the field to that date brilliantly well. It is therefore appropriate to quote him in some detail:

The first important work of discography is Schleman's *Rhythm on record.* This book is subtitled 'A who's who and register of recorded dance music, 1906–1936' and it was published in England by the periodical *Melody Maker* early in 1936. A few months later in the same year came the first edition of the French critic Delaunay's work *Hot discography.* It is interesting to compare these two pioneer compilations in the light of later developments, in the discographical field. Schleman is largely forgotten now, and his work has become a collector's item, but his approach had much to recommend it. The listings were arranged alphabetically by artist, from Aaronson's Commanders to Zutty (Singleton)'s Band. Although Schleman did not exclude blues artists, such as Lizzie Miles, Bobby Leecan, Sylvester Weaver and Victoria Spivey (all of whom were listed later only partially or not at all by Delauney), the sub-title of his work accurately describes his interest in detailing recorded dance music. Thus he includes along with various 'hot' artists, whom we are now accustomed to find in jazz discographies, the full output of such as Jack Hylton, George Olsen and other 'popular' dance band leaders of the day, including many British and American popular artists whom most jazz collectors would now find of absolutely no interest, but who, it should be noted, are still of some historical value. Additionally, Schleman planned and described his volume as 'A who's who' as well as a 'register'. Before the discographical listings of each artist, Schleman gives a short biography and thus foreshadowed Leonard Feather's *Encyclopedia of jazz* and the Panassie-Gautier *Dictionary of jazz*. In terms of discographical detail, Schleman is sadly wanting by later standards. His personnel listings and recording dates are for the most part collective ones and the tune titles are listed, not chronologically but alphabetically by record label, with a catalogue number following each. . . . Schleman was also uncritical of factual information reaching him and his book contains numerous major errors. He was outside the mainstream of 'hot' record research and his work never inspired later researchers as Delaunay's did, but it is interesting to speculate on the progress of discography if his principles of all-inclusiveness and biographical data had prevailed. Beyond its nostalgic interest *Rhythm on record* even today provides one of the best sources of information about the personnel, recordings and bookings of the popular dance groups of the 1920's.

The French critic Charles Delaunay, who has edited jazz journals and written an excellent life of Django Reinhardt, is also the 'father of jazz discography' and, as Sheatsley says above, he inspired the field. Undoubtedly the various and improving editions of *Hot discography* have proved to be vital in the beginnings of a scholarly approach to jazz music. Discography in jazz is the counterpart to bibliography in the literary field and Delaunay is owed a great debt by all researchers into the subject. Sheatsley continues:

Delaunay's approach was entirely different. As his title indicates . . . he was interested in 'Le jazz hot' and drew a sharp distinction between this and commercial or dance music. Furthermore he followed Panassie's classic view of the development of jazz, from the New Orleans pioneers up the River to Chicago, thence to New York, culminating in the large and small hot Negro bands of the 1930's with their white imitators, and his discography was deliberately ordered to show this development. Instead of listing the artists alphabetically, Delaunay adopted an historical approach—starting his book with King Oliver, the Original Dixieland Jazz Band, and the New Orleans Rhythm Kings; then proceeding to discographies of the great soloists—Armstrong, Dodds, Ladnier, etc., the great blues singers—Bessie Smith and Ma Rainey and pioneer large orchestras—Henderson, McKinney, Ellington, thence to Beiderbecke, the Chicagoans, the Nichols, Mole, Lang and Venuti combinations; Goodman, Teagarden and the Dorseys, and finally a miscellaneous selection of studio groups, ordered alphabetically by artist. As we shall see, this selective and doctrinaire approach was to have serious disadvantages, but despite Schleman's precedence chronologically and despite the weaknesses in his own approach, Charles Delaunay is the undoubted father of discography as we know it today. It was he who first saw and utilised the importance of master numbers and who from the beginning aimed at the ideal of listing each artist's work in matrix number order, with full personnels and recording-date for each session.

The 1936 edition was severely limited in this respect, but successive revisions in 1938, 1943, and especially in 1948, came closer to the ultimate goal, as new knowledge became available. Though the post-war edition was greatly expanded and the claim made that 'this work lists nearly all discovered recordings', Delaunay's approach still remained quite selective. In this 1948 edition, post 1930 artists are grouped alphabetically without regard to style, but the first half of the book still follows the historical chronological approach. As Delaunay says in his foreword 'Some readers might prefer for their own convenience a strictly alphabetical order, but that would destroy the historical aim of this work, which turns a simple enumeration of recordings into a fascinating account of the evolution of an art form.' It is true that Delaunay's selective emphasis on the major figures of early jazz history and his groupings of records into Chicago, New York and other such sections added glamour to the listings and did give a coherent if somewhat oversimplified picture of jazz development, but it is also true that this approach produced some notable omissions and distortions, e.g. all of the records on which each major artist appeared are listed under his name, even when he was merely a side-man or accompanist to others. . . . . For a decade or more Delaunay was the basic jazz discographer and his influence was pervasive. I must confess that I myself accepted his listings completely uncritically in those days!

Orin Blackstone, the American discographer, also played a significant part in documenting much of the elusive detail associated with early days of jazz recording. His *Index to jazz* is another standard work of discography and it is fortunate that this long out-of-print work has now been made available by University Microfilms in a paperbound Xerox facsimile edition. Paul Sheatsley says that:

It was Orin Blackstone in New Orleans in the years 1945–1948 who almost single-handed managed to complete the first attempt at a definitive listing of all records of jazz or blues interest. Blackstone's four part *Index to jazz* was ordered from A to Z, and as explained in his foreword 'because it was conceived as an index, this list follows a rigid alphabetical arrangement, according to the artists names' under which the records were originally issued.' . . . Blackstone set another important standard when he stated explicitly 'It is not the purpose of this index to evaluate in any way the records listed, except that they be of interest to the jazz collector.' One deficiency in Blackstone's work was his ordering of each artist's product by catalogue number rather than matrix number. This does not matter too much in most cases because the importance of the original index lies in the bare listings rather than in the richness of his discographical detail. Dates, personnels, master numbers and even instrumentation were often lacking, since Blackstone often had to rely solely on old catalogues, and no other information was available at the time, but where fuller details were known and sides from two different sessions were coupled, the ordering by release number resulted in awkward parenthetical notes to see some other date for the personnel on one of the sides. The first edition of the index was clearly announced as a trial run and the second edition was promised at an early date. Sure enough, only a year after the original part four appeared, part one of a new loose-leaf edition was mailed to subscribers. It was an impressive job. The original part one had been published in 1945; the new edition of A to E included all records issued during the intervening four years.

If Blackstone had been permitted but three more years of productive effort on the revised *Index to jazz* it is probable that his work would have become the standard reference for jazz discography up to the year 1950 . . . personal affairs forced his retirement from the field at this point and never again was it to be possible for one man to capture and publish the entire jazz catalog.

The major early British contribution to discography was the *Directory of recorded jazz and swing music* which is a basic, scholarly and useful work of reference which remains incomplete after six volumes and seven years of effort. It is often known as the *Jazz directory* and it is under this abbreviated title that Sheatsley discusses it in the following terms:

But England, the home of Schleman, had again picked up the discographical torch. Soon after Delaunay's 1948 edition was published and almost concurrently with the revision of Blackstone's part 1, appeared volume 1 of *Jazz directory* compiled by Dave Carey, Albert McCarthy, and Ralph Venables, a trio whose qualifications for the task were impeccable. Like Blackstone the *Directory* disclaimed a selective approach: 'We have admitted on the one hand Negro spiritual, gospel and "race" recordings (of obvious historical and sociological importance) and, on the other, an extremely liberal presentation of swing and be-bop, in order to reflect adequately the complete picture. . . . The non-inclusion of authentic calypso and hill-billy artists is regrettable . . . but insufficient research into their respective spheres had made it impossible to assess values at this time. . . . Commercial renderings have been included only where the prestige of the artist merits so doing or because soloists of value are featured. It seems certain that none would wish us to put in countless quasi-hot recordings by sundry aggregations, having no bearing on the subject.'

A comparison between the first volume of the *Directory* (covering letters A and B) and the first volume of Blackstone's revised *Index* leaves little to choose between them. Each has a few artists, issues, dates or master numbers which the other lacks, but they are remarkably similar. . . . The *Directory* is far better produced, neatly printed with lots of white space. The *Index* was photo off-set, mostly in double column format and presents a cluttered appearance. The loose-leaf idea so often recommended for discographies proved impractical (at least in my experience) since the pages gradually fell off like leaves as the volume received more and more handling. As 'C–D' and subsequent volumes of the *Directory* appeared this discography soon became indispensable to collectors. There was considerable delay in publishing the later volumes and the work was eventually abandoned with volume 6, K to L. The exceedingly high cost of production in such an attractive format and perhaps even more formidably the rising flood of new jazz labels and the bewildering output of jazz and blues material on long playing and 45 r.p.m. at that time caused this sad event. It might have been better to limit the *Directory's* objectives, say to 1948, aiming for comprehensiveness up to that date. There would then have been available perhaps by 1952 or even earlier, a complete general discography covering all artists from A to Z for the first 30 years of jazz recording.

Brian Rust's *Jazz records A to Z, 1897–1931* published by the author, first appeared in loose-leaf form in 1961 and was revised in hard cover in 1963. This is now the basic jazz discography for those years. Rust has little or no interest in post-1940 jazz but he is one of the most knowledgeable men in the world concerning recordings before that time and had a dogged determination to get it all into print. There are no doubt some errors in the work but it is impossible to imagine any new and independent effort to document the entire range of pre-1932 recordings. Rust is now further revising this work and a new edition is expected shortly. A further volume by this author, entitled *Jazz records, A–Z, 1932–1942*, appeared in 1965. This had 680 pages, listing everything available over the ten-year period and Rust has thus got down in two major volumes the results of a life-time study of the discography of jazz of this period. Associated with Rust is the work by John Godrich and Robert Dixon entitled *Blues and gospel records, 1902–1942*. This work complements Rust's own discographies and first appeared in 1964 with 765 pages. A revised edition appeared in 1969 with over 900 pages. Another major book in the blues field is *Blues records* by Leadbitter and Slaven published in 1968.

The last major discographical work to be completed is *Jazz records 1942–1962* by Jorgen Jepsen. The Danish discographer has supplemented Rust's second volume by attempting to list all details of all jazz records from 1942 to 1962. He has also supplemented Carey and McCarthy's *Jazz directory* and for this reason started his work with Volume 5 M–N. Volumes 6, 7 and 8 followed before Jepsen returned to complete volumes 1 to 4. His calculations went astray somewhat and the total set will consist of substantially more than the planned eight. In the later volumes Jepsen has widened his set limits, as can be seen from the bibliographical details given at the end of the chapter. This major discographical effort is already accepted as the standard work in the field.

A few further works deserve mention—the 6th edition of Delaunay with the collaboration of Kurt Mohr was published in France in 1951-52 under the title of *Hot discographie encyclopédique.* This was noteworthy because it marked a radical change in Delaunay's approach. He announced in his foreword that . . . 'This new discography in contrast to preceding editions, will be issued in several volumes. This splitting into parts has obliged us to abandon the procedure followed in previous discographies of arrangement in sections according to affinities in style and to adopt a strictly alphabetical classification,' and he adds . . . 'The object of discography is to try to cover the entire output of recordings by the musicians and orchestras without regard to the value of the recordings. A work such as this must therefore include a considerable number of discs which do not merit acquisition by a collector but which must appear in the listing.' Three volumes of *Hot discographie encyclopédique* appeared, bringing it alphabetically as far as Neal Hefti, but at that point publication ceased. The work was lagging behind and less complete than *Jazz directory* and undoubtedly failed to sell for that reason. In 1960 Albert J. McCarthy, who of course had been concerned with *Jazz directory*, made another notable contribution to discographical literature by the publication of *Jazz discography 1958.* The purpose of this beautifully printed 271-page work was clearly stated by McCarthy in his introduction. 'For some time it has been obvious to all engaged in discographical research in the jazz field that the sheer volume of new issues is making the task of compiling a complete work and jazz directory almost impossible. It is essential to document the new issues as they appear, or within a reasonable time of their release, or else one will forever be bogged down in the task of filing comparatively new editions to the list.' McCarthy attempted to list all items issued, including re-issues during the calendar year 1958, and he explicitly stated his intentions to compile future volumes on an annual basis. In fact for a time his journal *Jazz Monthly* listed in a supplement the monthly records which appeared. Another major contribution to continuing jazz discography is produced by McCarthy's rivals in the

British jazz magazine field. *Jazz Journal* publish the annual *Jazz catalogue* which is compiled by George Cherrington and Brian Knight. The standard and comprehensiveness of the work has improved tremendously since it commenced publication in 1960 and it includes all jazz and blues issued on British labels during the year. It is also valuable to the bibliographer since about one quarter of each volume is devoted to Colin Johnson's listings of books and articles on jazz. Coverage of this section extends beyond the purely jazz journals and this substantially adds to its value.

Typical, perhaps, of discographies limited by geographical area are Harry Nicolaussen's *Svensk jazzdiskografie* (1953) which covers Swedish records and Horst Lange's 650-page work *Die Deutsch Jazz Discographie* which was published in German in 1955.

A second major work by Lange was published in 1966. This was *Die Deutsche 78-er Discographie der Jazz-und Hot-Dance-Musik, 1903–1958* and it reflected the author's keen interest in early jazz and also in certain non-jazz orchestras. Lange feels that many of the latter have been overlooked by other discographical researchers. As the title implies, this book draws a line at the end of the 78 r.p.m. period and no long play records are included. The balance, from the purely jazz viewpoint, is distorted in some ways, as, for example, there are seventeen pages devoted to the work of Harry Roy and only six pages to Benny Goodman. This is a valuable contribution to the field and gives a good picture of jazz activity in Germany over 50 years.

Other discographical work has been of a limited nature in that it has applied to the work of one artist or group of artists. There has been a tremendous amount of activity in this field, much of it included in the periodical literature, but several books are worth selecting for mention here. The term bio-discography is used to indicate a work which gives the life of its subject in some detail before listing comprehensively all his recorded musical output. *King Joe Oliver* (1957) by Brian Rust and Walter Allen set a new standard for this art. This was a fully documented work of scholarship divided into three main sections, a bibliography and five appendices. The 43 pages of section one are straight biography while the brief section two assesses Oliver's work and influence. The discographical section consists of almost 100 pages and is exceptionally fine in its attention to detail. The bibliography includes references from 33 different publications and the appendices include lists of orchestra itineraries, an index of recorded titles and an index of musicians who worked with Oliver.

Other work of a similar excellent standard is by Howard Waters in his *Jack Teagarden's music: his career and recordings* (1960). This is a later volume in the Jazz Monographs series published by Water Allen which included the Allen/Rust book on Oliver. There is a useful bibliography and various indexes are a feature of a superb book. The work of Duke Ellington is documented fully in Luigi Sanfillipo's *General catalogue of Duke Ellington's recorded music.* This book contains all Ellington's output up to 1965. A further excellent example of bio-discography is Connor and Hicks' *B.G.—on the record* (1969), which originally appeared under the slightly different title of *B.G.—off the record* in 1958. This was by Connor alone and the new book is virtually a new work. A series of irregular discographical pamphlets of a good standard is edited by Ernie Edwards, a Californian, and some associates. Coverage is best on big band jazz and includes some lesser known artists and orchestras such as Les Brown and Jan Savitt. Another excellent series of discographical pamphlets averaging around 40 pages is produced by master discographer Jorgen Jepsen and some Danish friends. These include works on 'free' jazz, Dizzy Gillespie, John Coltrane, Basie, Monk, Lester Young and others and all are tidily produced and of a high standard discographically.

A project to compile and maintain a bibliography of jazz discographies has been instituted by Pete Moon and the British Institute of Jazz Studies. The aim is to list all discographies published since 1960 and details given include artist, compiler's name, format, source, publication date, etc. An interim listing appeared in *Jazz Studies,* vol. 2(3), pp. 44–48, 1968.

Books which are aimed more at the general listener to jazz music are the annotated record guides. The earliest, and still one of the best, is Ramsey and Smith's *Jazz record book* which appeared in 1942 with over 500 pages. Frederic Ramsey on his own produced a useful *Guide to long play jazz records* in 1954 and two other critical guides by John S. Wilson were published in America in the late 'fifties under the titles of *Collectors' jazz: modern* and *Collectors' jazz: traditional and swing.*

In Britain a paperback entitled *Recorded jazz: a critical guide* was published in 1958. It was written by Rex Harris and Brian Rust and was arranged alphabetically by band. It provided useful critical notes on records up to 1957 but in the traditional field only. The title is therefore somewhat misleading. A better example is *Jazz on record* (1960) by Charles Fox and others, which is a useful guide to collecting the basic records. A revised and expanded edition of this volume was published early in 1968. It is a joint effort by Albert McCarthy, Paul Oliver, Alun Morgan and Max Harrison and differs from the first edition in that it is not restricted to current issues on British labels.

Other guides which need to be mentioned, since they might well be overlooked, are the catalogues of the gramophone record companies. Complete issues usually appear annually and regular supplements are published to keep them up to date. Some companies issue special catalogues for jazz often with supplementary articles by jazz critics and sleeve note writers. *Jazz from Columbia* by George Avakian is a typical example of this type of publication.

Other aids to jazz collectors can be divided into two categories. One is the directory type of book which lists collectors' names, addresses and special interests and a useful American title which first appeared in 1942, and in a much enlarged second edition in 1949, was *Who's who in jazz collecting.* This was by William Love and Bill Rich and is now very out of date, but, since jazz collectors are a persistent and long-lived breed, not entirely useless.

The second category is typified by Andy Anderson's *Helpful hints to jazz collectors* (1957) and this book will be supplemented, and perhaps superseded, by Derek Langridge's *Your jazz collection.* In fact Langridge's book will be unique in its approach since it includes detailed guidance to the collector not only on the collecting of jazz records, books and other materials but practical advice on their classification, cataloguing and arrangement. This information is imparted by an expert since Langridge is principal lecturer at one of Britain's leading schools of librarianship. This same author's outline of a classification system for the literature of jazz was published in the British musical periodical *Brio* in 1967.

Compared to the discographical literature, the bibliographical side of jazz literature has been relatively neglected until very recent years. The first, and still the major, published work, is Alan Merriam and Robert Benford's *A bibliography of jazz* which was published in Philadelphia by the American Folklore Society in 1954.

It is the most comprehensive bibliography on the subject yet published and includes over 3,300 entries for books and periodical articles appearing before the end of 1950. The authors state that the work is not selective and entries are included which are both pro- and anti-jazz, well-written and ephemeral. Articles have been culled from both jazz and non-jazz magazines but the bibliography makes no claim to completeness. Rather is it to be regarded as a 'beginning towards the orderly gathering of the tremendous literature which has grown up around jazz music'. It is divided into three parts—the first and major section consists of entries arranged alphabetically by author and at the end of each a coding system, indicates broadly what subject is discussed in the reference. Thirty-two categories range from A and A (Analysis and appreciation) through to Tech (Technical equipment used in jazz).

The second section of the bibliography consists of a listing of magazines devoted wholly or in considerable part to jazz music. There are 113 entries in this section from all over the world. Many of the titles listed are now defunct. The third section consists of indexes to both subject and periodicals cited. This is a work of scholarship which is indispensable to any student of the jazz literature.

Another important work is *The literature of jazz*, a 63-page pamphlet by Robert C. Reisner, who was formerly on the staff of the New York Public Library and Curator at the Institute of Jazz Studies. The second revised and enlarged edition appeared in 1959 published by the New York Public Library and is a check list giving books on jazz (including fiction) listed under author (some 500 titles). There is also a separate list of background books and a selective list of some 850 periodical references. Reisner also includes probably the most comprehensive listing of periodicals devoted wholly or principally to jazz published throughout the world. It is interesting to compare the two editions of Reisner's work. The first edition of 1954 was sub-titled 'a preliminary bibliography' and its 53 pages were divided into three sections—books, journal articles and jazz magazines. The second edition divides the books section into books (on jazz) and background books. Also in the second edition all the journal references are selected from non-jazz magazines; this is different to the first edition. In neither edition is there any real subject approach although the compiler claims some via biographical references.

In Britain the pioneer bibliographical work was a selective *Readers' guide to books on jazz* compiled by J. R. Haselgrove and the present writer, which was published by the County Libraries Section of the Library Association in 1960. This was completely revised for a second edition by the same compilers in 1965. It is a selective listing of material on jazz arranged under the headings of general background, theory and criticism, biography, discographies and reference books, jazz literature, periodicals and a basic record collection. 160 books, 20 periodicals and 50 long-playing records are included. This 16-page guide is one of a series of similar bibliographies issued by the County Libraries Group (as it is now) of the British Library Association. A number of individual public libraries in Britain have issued short reading-lists on jazz and a particularly notable one appeared in 1963 from the Staffordshire County Library. It was a nine-page annotated and select list mainly aimed at young adults but extremely useful to anyone interested in the more important books on the music. Some

60 items are included, including a selection of tutors for learning to play the various instruments used in jazz. Bibliographies of jazz literature in Swedish and German appeared in 1964 in leading jazz journals in those countries. The *Svensk jazzbiografi* listed some 58 items of which 24 were translations from the English originals. The list was compiled by Lars Kleberg and appeared in *Orkester Journalen,* for December 1964. The magazine *Jazz Podium* included a *Bibliographie der deutschsprachigen Jazz-Blues und Spiritualliteratur* by Carl Gregor Herzog zu Mecklenburg. This is a list of 113 items, of which 22 only are translations from the English. Separately published bibliographies of jazz literature have been issued in pamphlet form in France and the Netherlands. *La litteratur du jazz* by Jacques Chaumier is probably the most comprehensive bibliography in the French language and is arranged in two sections. The first section is arranged by author and the second under broad subject headings. There are 232 entries altogether, many of them briefly annotated. Arie Elings' *Bibliografie van de Nederlandse jazz* was compiled as a partial requirement for a university degree and is the only jazz bibliography in Dutch. The 157 references are restricted to jazz in Holland and the main section is arranged in a classified arrangement. There are indexes under both author and subject.

Finally in this bibliographical section there are several works of background interest to the study of jazz music. *A select bibliography of music in Africa* was compiled by L. J. P. Gaskin of the library of the International African Institute and published by that body in 1965, and its 83 pages provide excellent listings in which general works are followed by items listed under the names of individual countries. Comprehensive indexes of authors etc. complete the work. A recent bibliography on *The Negro in America* was published in 1966 by Harvard University Press. The compiler of this 190-page work is Elizabeth Miller. Somewhat more relevant to our study is *Ethnomusicology and folk-music: an international bibliography of dissertations and theses* which was compiled by jazz bibliographer Alan

Merriam with Frank Gillis and published in 1966. This has
148 pages and was published by the Society for Ethnomusicology.

BIBLIOGRAPHY

AASLUND, B. H. *The 'wax works' of Duke Ellington.* Stockholm,
Foliotryck, 1954. Discography of Ellington records up to 1954.
ALLEN, W. C. and RUST, B. A. L. *King Joe Oliver.* Stanhope,
N.J., Walter C. Allen, 1955. (Jazz Monographs No. 1.) Bio-
discography of leading jazz cornet player and band-leader. A
valuable work.
—— —— London, Jazz Book Club, 1957.
—— —— London, Sidgwick and Jackson, 1958.
ANDERSON, A. *Helpful hints to jazz collectors: combined with
jazz men and their records.* Baraboo, Wisconsin, Andoll, 1957.
Includes discography and biography.
AVAKIAN, G. *Jazz from Columbia: a complete jazz catalog.*
New York, Columbia Records, 1956. Record company publica-
tion listing jazz records linked by brief essays on various jazz
styles.
BANNISTER, L. H. *International jazz collectors' directory.*
Malvern, Worcs., The author, 1948.
BEDWELL, S. F. *A Glenn Miller discography and biography:*
edited and with additional material by Geoffrey E. Butcher.
London, Glenn Miller Appreciation Society, 1955.
—— —— Rev. ed. London, Glenn Miller Appreciation Society,
1956.
BERG, I. and YEOMANS, I. *Trad: an A–Z who's who of the British
traditional jazz scene.* London, Foulsham, 1962. Covers the
period 1947–1962 but of little permanent value.
BLACKSTONE, O. *Index to jazz.* 4 volumes. New Orleans,
Gordon Gullickson, 1947.
—— —— Loose leaf ed. IV. New Orleans, The author? 195–
—— —— London, University Microfilms, 196? Paperback Xerox
edition.
—— *The Jazzfinder '49.* New Orleans, The author, 1949.
CAREY, D. and McCARTHY, A. J. comps. *The Directory of
recorded jazz and swing music.* 6 volumes. Volume 1: A–B.
Fordingbridge, Hants., Delphic Press, 1950. Volume 2: C–D.
Fordingbridge, Hants., Delphic Press, 1950. 2nd ed. London,
Cassell, 1955. Volume 3: E–G. Fordingbridge, Hants., Delphic

Press, 1951. 2nd ed. London, Cassell, 1956. Volume 4: G–I. Fordingbridge, Hants., Delphic Press, 1952. 2nd ed. London, Cassell, 1957. Volume 5: J–KIRK. London, Cassell, 1955. Volume 6: KIRK–LONG. London, Cassell, 1957. Basic and scholarly work which ends with the entry for Longshaw (vol. 6). Continued by Jepsen (q.v.) and McCarthy in *Jazz discography* (1960).

CHARTERS, S. B. *Jazz: New Orleans, 1885–1957, an index to the Negro musicians of New Orleans.* Bellville, W. C. Allen, 1958 (Jazz monographs no. 2). Discography.

—— *New Orleans, 1885–1963, an index to the Negro musicians of New Orleans.* New York, Oak Publications, 1963.

CHAUMIER, J. *La litteratur du jazz: essai de bibliographie.* Le Mans, The author, 1963. (In French.) 232 entries many briefly annotated.

CHERRINGTON, G. *and* KNIGHT, B. *eds. Jazz catalogue: a discography of all jazz releases issued in Great Britain.* London, Jazz Journal, 1960– (annual in progress). Includes a complete bibliography by Colin A. Johnson.

CONNOR, D. R. *B.G.—off the record: a bio-discography of Benny Goodman.* Fairless Hills, Pa., Gaildonna, 1958.

CONNOR, D. R. *and* HICKS, WARREN, W. *B.G.—on the record: a bio-discography of Benny Goodman.* New Rochelle, N.Y., Arlington House, 1969.

CUSACK, T. *Jelly Roll Morton: an essay in discography.* London, Cassell, 1952.

DAUER, A. *and* LONGSTREET, S. *Knaur's jazz lexicon.* Munich, Droemeitsche verlagsanstalt, 1957. (In German.)

—— *Encyclopédie du jazz.* Translation by J. Bureau. Paris, Aimery Somogy, 1958.

DAVIES, J. H. *Musicalia: sources of information in music.* London, Pergamon Press and J. Curwen, 1966. Rather weak on jazz. Chapter 11 (pages 109–122) is devoted to the folk-singer and jazzman.

DAVIES, J. R. T. *The music of Thomas 'Fats' Waller.* London, Friends of Fats, 1953.

DECCA RECORD COMPANY LTD. *Complete catalogue of London Origins of Jazz records.* London, Decca Record Company Ltd., 1957.

—— *Complete catalogue: records issued by the Decca Record Company Ltd. and Vogue Records Ltd.* London, Decca Record Company Ltd. Annual. Supplementary catalogues issued every four months.

—— Complete catalogue of R.C.A. Victor, R.C.A. Victoria, R.C.A. Camden records. London, Decca Record Company Ltd. Annual. Supplementary catalogues issued every four months.

—— Jazz on L.P.'s: a collector's guide to jazz. Rev. ed. London, Decca Record Company, 1956.

—— Jazz on 78's: a guide to the many examples of classic jazz. London, Decca Record Company, 1954.

DELAUNAY, C. Hot discographie. Paris, Hot Jazz, 1936. (In French.) Discographer's 'Bible'—at least for the earlier decades of jazz recording.

—— —— 2nd ed. Paris, Hot Jazz, 1938. (In French.)

—— —— 3rd ed. New York, Commodore Record Co., 1943.

—— —— 1943. Paris, Collection du Hot Clubs de France, 1944.

—— New hot discography: the standard directory of recorded jazz. Edited by Walter E. Schaap and George Avakian. New York, Criterion Music Corporation, 1948.

—— —— New York, Wehman, 1963.

DELAUNAY, C. and MOHR, K. Hot discographie encylopédique. 3 volumes. Paris, Editions Jazz Disques. Volume 1: A–B, 1951. Volume 2: C–El, 1952. Volume 3: El–H, 1953. (In French.)

EDWARDS, E. ed. Big bands. 2 volumes. Whittier, Calif., Jazz Discographies Unlimited, 196?

—— Bill Harris discography. Whittier, Calif., Jazz Discographies Unlimited, 1966.

—— Dizzy Gillespie big bands 1945–1950. Whittier, Calif., Jazz Discographies Unlimited, 1966.

—— Jimmie Lunceford. Whittier, Calif., Jazz Discographies Unlimited, 196?

—— Les Brown and his Band of Renown. Whittier, Calif., Jazz Discographies Unlimited, 196?

EDWARDS, E., HALL, G. and KORST, B. eds. Charlie Barnet and his orchestra. Whittier, Calif., Jazz Discographies Unlimited, 196?

ELECTRICAL AND MUSICAL INDUSTRIES LTD. Alphabetical catalogue of E.M.I. records: records available and issued up to and including . . . London, E.M.I. Annual.

ELINGS, A. Bibliografie van de Nederlandse jazz. Nijmegen, Stichting Algemene Openbare Bibliotheek, 1966. (In Dutch.) 157 references limited to jazz in Holland.

FAIRCHILD, R. Discography of Art Hodes. Ontario, Calif., The author, 1962.

FEATHER, L. The encyclopedia of jazz. Foreword by Duke Ellington. New York, Horizon Press, 1955. Major reference book on jazz. Over two thirds of the work is devoted to biographies of musicians.

—— —— London, A. Barker, 1956.

—— —— The new edition of the Encyclopedia of jazz revised, enlarged and brought up to date. New York, Horizon Press, 1960.

—— —— London, A. Barker, 1961.

—— *The encyclopedia of jazz in the Sixties.* New York, Horizon Press, 1967. Supplements the earlier encyclopedia and is particularly strong on the younger musicians.

—— *Encylopedia yearbook of jazz.* New York, Horizon Press, 1956.

—— —— London, A. Barker, 1957.

—— *New yearbook of jazz.* New York, Horizon Press, 1958.

—— —— London, A. Barker, 1959.

FOX, C., GAMMOND, P. *and* MORGAN, A. *Jazz on record : a critical guide ; with additional material by A. Korner.* London, Hutchinson, 1960. Useful for collecting the basic records but now out of date. Updated by McCarthy et al. *Jazz on record* (1968).

FRY, A., KAPLAN, M. *and* LOVE, W. C. *Who's who in jazz collecting.* Nashville, Hemphill Press, 1942.

GANFIELD, J. *Books and periodical articles on jazz in America from 1926–1934.* New York, Columbia University School of Library Service, 1934. Typewritten pamphlet—possibly the first separately issued bibliography on the subject.

GASKIN, L. J. P. *A select bibliography of music in Africa : compiled at the International African Institute.* London, International African Institute, 1965.

GILLIS, F. *and* MERRIAM, A. P. *comps. Ethnomusicology and folkmusic : an international bibliography of dissertations and theses.* Middletown, Conn., Society for Ethnomusicology and Wesleyan University Press, 1966. (Special series in ethnomusicology volume 1.)

GODRICH, J. *and* DIXON, R. M. W. *Blues and gospel records, 1902–1942.* London, B. Rust. Basic discography in its field.

—— —— 2nd ed. revised. London, Storyville Publications, 1969.

GOLD, R. S. *Jazz lexicon : an A–Z dictionary of jazz terms in the vivid idiom of America's most successful non-conformist minority.* New York, Knopf, 1964. Accent is on the sociological aspects of jazz. Includes bibliography (pages 353–363).

HALL, G. *ed. Jan Savitt and his Top Hatters.* Whittier, Calif., Jazz Discographies Unlimited, 196?

86   The Literature of Jazz

—— Nat 'King' Cole. Whittier, Calif., Jazz Discographies Un-
limited, 196?
HARRIS, H. M. *A jazz bibliography.* (*In* BLACKSTONE, O. *The
jazzfinder '49*, pp. 129–142.)
HARRIS, R. *and* RUST, B. *Recorded jazz : a critical guide.* London,
Penguin Books, 1958. Traditional jazz only is covered.
HARVEY, C. M. *and* RUST, B. *The Al Bowlly discography.*
London, B. Rust, 1965.
HASELGROVE, J. R. *and* KENNINGTON, D. *comps. Readers'
guide to books on jazz.* London, Library Association County
Libraries Section, 1960. Brief selective list.
—— —— 2nd ed. London, Library Association County Libraries
Group, 1965.
HERZOG ZU MECKLENBURG, C. G. *Bibliographie der deutschsprachigen Jazz, Blues- und Spiritualliteratur. Jazz Podium,* v.
13 (3), 1964, pp. 66–68. (In German.) Comprehensive listing of
jazz books in German.
JEPSEN, J. G. *Jazz records: a discography.* Volume 1: A–Bl,
1942–1965. Holte, Denmark, Knudsen, 1966. Volume 2: Bl–Co,
1942–1965. Holte, Denmark, Knudsen, 1966. Volume 3: Co–Gl,
1942–1965. Holte, Denmark, Knudsen, 1967. Volume, 4A:
Gl–Goo, 1942–1967. Holte, Denmark, Knudsen, 1968. Volume
5: M–N, 1942–1962, Copenhagen, Nordisk Tidskrift Forlag,
1963. Volume 6: O–R, 1942–1962. Copenhagen, Nordisk
Tidskrift Forlag, 1963. Volume 7: S–Te, 1942–1962. Holte,
Denmark, Knudsen, 1964. Volume 8: Te–Z, 1942–1962, Holte,
Denmark, Knudsen, 1965. Major discographical reference
work. To be completed in further volumes.
JORGENSEN, J. *and* WIEDEMANN, E. *Mosaik-jazzlexicon.*
Hamburg, Musaik verlag, 1966. (In German.) Includes compre-
hensive bibliography.
KLEBERG, L. *Svensk jazzbiografi. Orkester Journalen,* Dec.
1964, pp. 47–48. (In Swedish.) Lists books on jazz published in
Sweden.
LAADE, W. *Jazz-lexicon.* Stuttgart, Verlag Gerd Hatje, 1953. (In
German.)
LANGE, H. *Die Deutsche Jazz Discographie ; eine geschichte der
jazz auf Schallplatten von 1902 bis 1955.* Berlin, Bote and G.
Bock, 1955. (In German.)
—— *Die Deutsche 78-er Discographie der Jazz- und Hot-Dance-
Musik 1903–1958.* Berlin, Colloquium Verlag, 1966. (In German.)
LANGRIDGE, D. W. 'Classifying the literature of jazz', *Brio,*
v. 4 (1), 1967, pp. 2–6. Suggests that most established classi-

fication schemes are totally unsuitable for classifying the jazz literature and indicates how the *British Catalogue of Music* schedules might be usefully adapted.

—— 'Jazz and libraries', *Library World,* Mar. 1966, p. 260. Discusses the inadequacy of jazz record and literature provision in British public libraries.

—— *Your jazz collection.* London, Bingley, 1970. A comprehensive guide to the collecting of jazz records, books and other materials and to their classification, cataloguing and arrangement.

LEADBITTER, M. *and* SLAVEN, NEIL. *Blues records, January 1943 to December 1966.* London, Hanover Books, 1968.

LOVE, W. C. *and* RICH, B. *Who's who in jazz collecting.* 2nd ed. Nashville, The authors, 1949. Revised edition of FRY, A., KAPLAN, M. *and* LOVE, W. C. *Who's who in jazz collecting* (q.v.).

LUCAS, J. *Basic jazz on long play.* Northfield, Minn., Carleton College, 1954.

—— *The great revival on long play.* Northfield, Minn., Carleton Jazz Club, Carleton College, 1957.

McCARTHY, A. J. *Comp. Jazz discography: an international discography of recorded jazz including blues, gospel and rhythm and blues.* Part 1. 1958. London, Cassell, 1960. An attempt to continue the work started in *Directory of recorded jazz.* Part 1 was the only part published but McCarthy published discographical material in a supplement to his journal *Jazz monthly.*

McCARTHY, A. J., OLIVER, P., MORGAN, A. *and* HARRISON, M. *Jazz on record : a critical guide to the first 50 years, 1917–1967.* London, Hanover Books, 1968. Up-dates *Jazz on record* (1960) by C. Fox *et al.*

—— —— New York, Oak Publications, 1968.

MASSAGLI, L. *and others. Duke Ellington's story on records, 1923–1931.* Milan, Musica Jazz, 1966. Discography. (Series in progress.)

MERRIAM, A. P. *and* BENFORD, R. J. *A bibliography of jazz.* Philadelphia, American Folklore Society, 1954. Basic work including over 3,300 entries published before 1951.

MILLER, E. W. *comp. The Negro in America: a bibliography.* Cambridge, Harvard University Press, 1966.

MOON, P. 'Bibliography of discographies', *Jazz Studies,* v. 2 (3), 1968, pp. 44–48. Interim listing of separately published discographies covering the work of particular artists. Includes work in progress. It is not informative in bibliographical detail.

NICOLAUSSON, H. *Svensk jazzdiskografi.* Stockholm, Nordiska musikforlaget, 1953. (In Swedish.) Discography.

OLIVER, J. ed. *Jazz classic: an album of personalities from the world of jazz.* London, Tolgate Press, 1962. Album of photographs.

PANASSIE, H. *Discographie critique des meilleurs disques de jazz.* Paris, Laffont, 1958. (In French.)

—— 'Jazz' (*in* GROVE, *Dictionary of music and musicians.* 5th ed. 1954. Volume 4, pp. 599–605). Adequate coverage of traditional and mainstream styles of jazz. Bibliography.

—— *144 hot jazz Bluebird and Victor records.* Camden, N.J., Radio Corporation of America, 1939.

—— *Petit guide pour une discothèque de jazz.* Paris, Laffont, 1955. (In French.)

PANASSIE, H. *and* GAUTIER, M. *Dictionnaire du jazz.* Paris, Laffont, 1954. (In French.)

——*Dictionary of jazz.* Translated by Desmond Flower. London, Cassell, 1956.

—— *Guide to jazz.* Boston, Houghton Mifflin, 1956. American version of *Dictionnaire du jazz* (1954).

RAMSEY, F. *A guide to long play jazz records.* New York, Long Player Publications, 1954.

RAMSEY, F. *and* SMITH, C. E. *The jazz record book.* New York, Smith and Durrell, 1942. Valuable guide to earlier recordings.

REISNER, R. G. *The literature of jazz.* New York, New York Public Library, 1954. Checklist.

—— —— *a selective bibliography.* 2nd ed. revised and enlarged. New York, New York Public Library, 1959. This edition includes approximately 500 book titles on jazz, 850 journal references and a select list of background books. Also lists some 125 jazz magazines.

ROSE, A. *and* SOUCHON, E. *New Orleans jazz: a family album.* Baton Rouge, Louisiana State University Press, 1967. Useful guide to New Orleans musicians.

ROSENKRANTZ, T. *Swing photo album.* Copenhagen, The author, 1939.

—— *Swing photo album, 1939.* 2nd ed. Lowestoft, Suffolk, Scorpion Press, 1964.

ROWE, J. *and* WATSON, T. *Junkshoppers discography.* London, Jazz Tempo Publications, 1945. Guide to pseudonymous jazz bands.

RUST, B. *Jazz records A–Z 1897–1931.* London, The author, 1961. Basic reference work on its period.

—— —— 2nd ed. London, The author, 1963.

—— *Jazz records A–Z 1932–1942*. London, The author, 1965. Basic reference work on the period.

SANFILIPPO, L. *General catalogue of Duke Ellington's recorded music,* Palermo, New Jazz Society, 1964. Discography. Lists 1,472 titles which are arranged in alphabetical order and referred back to the discographical section. Also included are sections on transcription, both radio and television, V-discs and film. Running times of records are also given where known. This book supplements Aaslund, *The waxworks of Duke Ellington* (1954).

SCHLEMAN, H. R. *Rhythm on record : a who's who and register of recorded dance music, 1906–1936.* London, Melody Maker, 1936.

SCHOLES, P. 'Jazz' (*in OXFORD companion to music.* London, Oxford University Press, 9th ed. 1954). Worthless article which is inaccurate and patronising.

SEIBER, M. *and* FOX, C. 'Jazz' (*in CHAMBERS encyclopaedia.* London, Pergamon Press, 1966). Useful article with very brief bibliography.

SEMEONOFF, B. *Record collecting : a guide for beginners, with a chapter on collecting jazz records by Alexander Ross.* Chislehurst, Kent, Oakwood Press, 1949.

—— —— 2nd ed. rev. South Godstone, Surrey, Oakwood Press, 1951.

SHAPIRO, N. *ed. Popular music : an annotated index of American popular songs.* New York, Adrian Press. Volume 1: 1950–1959, 1964. Volume 3: 1960–1964, 1967. Volume 2: 1940–1949, 1965. Volume 4: 1930–1939, 1968. Comprehensive coverage of field including rhythm and blues, country and western, jazz, folk music and film, theatre and television tunes. Each entry includes copyright dates, full names of authors, composers and current publishers, details of first and best-selling records and performers who introduced or became identified with the songs. Arrangement is alphabetical by year with indexes of titles and publishers.

SHEATSLEY, P. B. 'A quarter century of jazz discography', *Record Research,* No. 58, Feb. 1964, pp. 3–6. A valuable and comprehensive survey of discographical literature.

SPARKE, M. *and others. Kenton on Capitol : a discography compiled with the co-operation of Capitol Records, Inc.* Hounslow, Middlesex,The author,1966. Comprehensive listing of Kenton's recorded work arranged chronologically from 1941 to date.

STAFFORDSHIRE COUNTY LIBRARY. *Jazz: a selection of books.* Stafford, Staffordshire County Library, 1963. (Books for young adults no. 2.) 60 entries.

STOCK, D. *photographer. Jazz street: with an introduction from and commentary by Nat Hentoff.* New York, Doubleday, 1960.

—— —— London, Deutsch, 1960.

—— —— London, Jazz Book Club, 1961.

TENOT, F. *and* CARLS, P. *Dictionnaire du jazz.* Parls, Larousse, 1967. (*Les dictionnaires de l'homme du xxe siècle.*) (In French.)

TESTONI, G. C. *Enciclopedia del jazz.* Milan, Messaggerie Musicali, 1953. (In Italian.)

WATERS, H. J. *Jack Teagarden's music: his career and recordings.* Stanhope, N.J., Allen, 1960. (Jazz monographs no. 3.) Excellent example of bio-discography. Bibliography.

WILBRAHAM, R. *Milt Jackson: a discography and biography (including recordings made with the Modern Jazz Quartet).* London, Frognal Bookshop, 1968.

WILLIAMS, M. T. 'Jazz' (*in ENCYCLOPAEDIA* Britannica. 1966. Volume 12, pp. 980–982). Useful informed article including discography of some significant jazz records of all styles. Brief bibliography.

WILSON, J. *Collectors' jazz: traditional and swing.* Philadelphia, Lippincott, 1958. Critical discography of long-playing records.

WILSON, J. *Collectors' jazz: modern.* Philadelphia, Lippincott, 1959. Critical discography of long-playing records.

CHAPTER 6

THE PERIODICAL LITERATURE

The periodical literature of jazz music is extremely poorly documented and in this and other ways compares closely with the literary field. In the jargon of jazz, it is the 'jazz mag', which is frequently produced under the auspices of a small group of like-minded individuals, appears more or less frequently for a year or two, and then dies. Since institutions such as libraries often wait to see if a journal is going to have significance before they acquire it, the jazz magazine often ceases publication without files being kept. Many of the publishers of these 'passing' journals either ignore or are unaware of legal deposit laws in their various countries, and thus they are never documented in any way. Occasionally files are held in private hands but access to these is obviously at best extremely limited.

In Britain many never appear in the *British National Bibliography,* and, as D. W. Langridge pointed out in an article in *Library World,* the position in Britain regarding publicly available sets of journals is bad. The *London Union List of Periodicals* has virtually nothing to offer—not even a single set of *Esquire* which has published many good articles on jazz. The Central Music Library in London has nothing except a three-year file of *Jazz Journal,* a monthly which commenced publication in 1948. The British Museum, which is purely a reference collection, has only about 12 examples of the genre and most of these are incomplete sets. Since Reisner in 1959 listed 125 journals, current and lapsed, this kind of coverage is pathetic. For the reasons mentioned above, it is extremely difficult to estimate how many specialist jazz journals have appeared since, but an intelligent guess would place the figure at around 200–300. This does not, of course, include the writings on jazz in newspapers and general periodicals, a section of the literature which is fairly substantial and in some cases very important. The American journal *Esquire*, as mentioned earlier, has long featured articles on jazz in its pages as has *Ebony, Playboy, Saturday Review* and *New Yorker.* Short pieces from the latter (by jazz critic Whitney Balliett) have appeared in book form and were referred to in Chapter 4. The American daily press has also featured regular articles on jazz music, such as the writings of John S. Wilson in the *New York Times.* In Britain the counterpart of this influential newspaper *The Times* has, even in its staider days, printed regular jazz criticism and also often (and sometimes surprisingly) includes obituary notices of even the most obscure jazz musicians. Other British newspapers are also relatively generous in jazz coverage and some distinguished critics prognosticate in their columns. Philip Larkin, librarian and poet, writes for the *Daily Telegraph* and a collection of the pieces published between 1961 and 1968 in that newspaper were produced in book form early in 1970 under the title *All what jazz* (see also bibliography to chapter 4).

Benny Green, ex-jazz musician turned critic, writes for the *Observer,* and other substantial newspapers like the *Sunday Times,* the *Yorkshire Post* and the *Guardian* have their regular well-informed pundits. Worthy of a mention before leaving the general periodicals published in Britain is the pioneering jazz journalism of the *New Statesman.* Several articles by music critic W. J. Turner appeared in its pages in the early 1920's and the tradition has been maintained in more recent years by Constant Lambert and Francis Newton, whose book published in 1959 was referred to in Chapter 1. The *Gramophone*, which was founded in 1923, is the leading British musical periodical of its type and is devoted mainly to classical European music and the technical problems of sound reproduction. It has also an impressive panel of jazz record reviewers and consequently some of the best reviews appear in its pages.

Jazz magazines proper divide broadly into four main categories with some inevitable overlapping between these groups. As might be expected, there is a tremendous variation in quality of production and content. The journals which are aimed at the widest readership, and can be loosely grouped together because they usually follow an editorial formula of feature articles, news, book and record reviews and plenty of photographs, are perhaps the aristocrats of the jazz magazine world. This group includes the American *Jazz* (now *Jazz and Pop*) and *Downbeat,* the British *Jazz Monthly* and *Jazz Journal,* the Swedish *Orkester Journalen,* the German *Jazz Podium* and the Canadian *Coda.* There are others of a similar quality throughout the world but these quoted are all good examples of the breed. They are all mostly 'pure' in that they exclude coverage of all material outside the jazz sphere. *Downbeat* is a bi-weekly magazine (which also appears in a Japanese edition) and it has been one of the most influential and reliable magazines in the jazz field, since its inception in 1933. It circulates internationally to about 40,000 readers and is indexed in *Music Index. Jazz Journal,* one of the two leading British journals, has been described as probably the finest all-round jazz magazine in the world. This was the verdict of an editor of a rival American journal. It covers the whole field of jazz in an adult and responsible manner, and many articles of permanent value have appeared in its pages since its commencement in 1948. It is also indexed by *Music Index* and, unusually for a jazz magazine, publishes an annual index to itself. Albert McCarthy's *Jazz Monthly* (1954 to date), with its scholarly articles, excellent reviews and regular discographical features, is probably the main reading of the British jazz intellectual. It is a first-class journal with an international reputation which has recently improved its physical presentation. Between 1962 and 1966 it included a supplement *Jazz Records* which listed jazz record releases of the month. Another useful journal is *Stonyville* which first appeared in 1965. It is published bi-monthly in London and is neatly produced with a mixture of discographical information and general articles. It has a special trading section paged separately with lists of records for sale.

Canada's leading magazine *Coda* has developed over the years since its birth in 1958 into a first-class publication. It appears bi-monthly and has world-wide correspondents who contribute regularly to its pages. An important German language magazine is Dieter Zimmerle's *Jazz Podium* which has appeared monthly since 1952. It circulates widely in both East and West Germany as well as Austria and Switzerland. A major influence in the Scandinavian jazz world is *Orkester Journalen* which has a record of continuous publication since 1933. This is a considerable achievement in a publishing field where one would estimate the average life of a magazine to be about 3–4 years. These journals are all current but one or two important and influential defunct magazines need to be mentioned. The short-lived *Jazz Review* (1958–1961) was edited by Nat Hentoff and Martin T. Williams and was perhaps the best jazz periodical produced in the United States. It was authoritative, academic and perhaps a little too serious but the contributions of a high standard which appeared in its pages included a great deal of permanent value to the jazz student. As mentioned in Chapter 4, *Jazz panorama* (1962) is a collection of these essays. Another important journal was *Record Changer* which flourished in the 1940's and early 1950's. In its May 1948 issue it included a complete index of all articles appearing in its pages from the first issue in August 1942 up to December 1947.

A larger group, but much less influential, are the purely local jazz magazines. These cover the activities of local personalities in depth, but most of their material is ephemeral and of little permanent significance. *The Second Line* which is produced irregularly by the New Orleans Jazz Club, is a better than average example of the species. This has been published since 1950 and includes articles of wider interest as well as the local news items. Other examples of lesser repute are *Hip* the Milwaukee jazz letter, *Jazz Times* (London) and *Just Jass* (Birmingham, U.K.).

A third specialised group are the discographical magazines which circulate to a small number of enthusiasts often spread through many countries. These magazines usually consist of discographical listings and a few articles. They seem to merge and split up very frequently. Typical examples are *Matrix* (which incorporated its rival *Discophile* in 1958). This is a bi-monthly record research magazine which has approximately 20 pages to each issue and is extremely useful in its specialised field. It has been published in Britain since 1954 and circulates internationally to some 300 readers. Like one of its American counterparts *Record Research* (and its subsidiary *Blues Research*), it is indexed in *Music Index*. *Record Research*, which is subtitled 'the magazine of record statistics and information', appears about nine times each year. It is comprised mainly, though not entirely, of jazz material and usually includes several articles as well as pages of discography and lists of records for auction. *Blues Unlimited*, a British journal, concentrates on the blues field and has a strong list of contributors. According to its editor 'it covers all forms of Negro blues, gospel and rhythm and blues from 1920 to the present day'. It publishes an index to itself.

Lastly there are magazines which are purely vehicles for the buying and selling of jazz records. Some are produced by record shops (e.g. *Record Finder* (U.S.A.) and *Goodchild's Jazz Bulletin* (U.K.)) but probably the most used and widest known is *Vintage Jazz Mart* which appears monthly and contains some 80 pages per issue. It circulates internationally and includes much otherwise unobtainable material. It is invaluable to the true collector but because of the tiny print is extremely difficult to read with the naked eye!

Another important title worth mentioning which does not fit into any of the above categories is the British *Melody Maker*. It has covered jazz in its pages since 1926 but as part of a wider interest in the popular music and entertainment field. A weekly with an 80,000 circulation, it has always been valuable for its current news.

The appeal of jazz to a world-wide audience is well demonstrated by a study of the periodical literature, and publications appear regularly in most languages and many countries. Apart from the more obvious ones there are magazines in Polish, Danish, Finnish, Dutch, Norwegian, Icelandic and Italian. Continental Europe has a long history of an intellectual and semi-intellectual interest in jazz since the early days of Robert Goffin and Hugues Panassie. Journals in French and German particularly have been appearing for many years.

LIST OF PERIODICALS

AMERICAN FOLK MUSIC OCCASIONAL. U.S.A. 1965–.
AMERICAN JAZZ REVIEW. U.S.A. 1944–?
ARIA JAZZ. (In Spanish.) Spain.
AUSTRALIAN JAZZ QUARTERLY. Australia. 1946–.
BAND LEADERS. U.S.A. 1942?
BASIN STREET. U.S.A. 1945.
BILLBOARD. (Formerly titled *Billboard Music Week.*) U.S.A. 1961–.
BLUES RESEARCH. U.S.A. 1959–. A subsidiary publication of *Record Research* (q.v.) devoted entirely to blues discography with few articles or record reviews. Consists almost entirely of discographical lists.
BLUES UNLIMITED : the journal of the Blues Appreciation Society. U.K. 1963–. Duplicated discographical magazine—according to a well-known critic A. J. McCarthy 'the finest magazine of its type'. Contains general articles on the blues plus biographical material on artists and the usual book and record reviews and discographical material. According to its editor it covers 'all forms of Negro blues, gospel and rhythm and blues from 1920 to the present day'. Also a regular column devoted to 'Cajun' music—the only column of its kind in the world. It has a strong list of contributors and agents in seven countries. Publishes an index to itself.
BLUES WORLD. U.K. 1965–.
BRIO. U.K. 1964–. Occasional articles and book reviews of jazz interest.
BRITISH INSTITUTE OF JAZZ STUDIES NEWSLETTER. U.K. 1966–. Duplicated news-sheet designed to report to members of the Institute on developments in its activities.
BULLETIN DU HOT CLUB DE FRANCE. (In French.) France.
BULLETIN DU HOT CLUB DU GENEVE: (In French.) Switzerland. 1950–.
CAHIERS DU JAZZ. (In French.) France. 1959–.
CLEF. U.S.A. 1946–?
CLIMAX. U.S.A. 1955–.
CODA: Canada's jazz magazine. Canada. 1958–. Canada's

leading jazz magazine includes news articles from various parts of the world plus a good section of record reviews.
COLLECTOR. Italy.
COLLETZIONE DI MUSICA JAZZ. (In Italian.) Italy. 1960–.
CRESCENDO: a monthly music magazine. U.K. 1962–. Not strictly a jazz magazine though containing a good proportion of interest to the jazz enthusiast. Aimed perhaps mainly at the amateur and semi-professional musician both jazz and non-jazz. Much of the advertising is directed to this group and several articles in each issue deal with instrumental technique —a thing never found in the 'pure' jazz magazine.
DISCOGRAPHICAL FORUM. U.K. 1960–1961.
DISCOGRAPHY. U.K. 1942–1946.
DISCOPHILE. U.K. 1948–1958. Pioneer discographical journal.
DISCOTECA: rivisto di dischi e musica. (In Italian.) Italy. 1959–.
DOCTOR JAZZ. (In Dutch.) Covers traditional jazz. Netherlands.
DOWNBEAT: the bi-weekly music magazine. (Also appears in Japanese.) U.S.A. 1934–. An internationally circulating magazine containing news, feature articles and reviews. One of the longest established journals, it is also one of the most influential and reliable American magazines in the jazz field. Indexed *Music Index.*
DOWNBEAT YEAR BOOK. U.S.A. 1954–.
DRUMMER. (In German.) Germany.
EBONY. U.S.A. 1945–. The leading picture magazine aimed at the American Negro market.
ESQUIRE. U.S.A. 1933–. This magazine has regularly published items by leading jazz critics such as Nat Hentoff, Leonard Feather, John Clellon Holmes, Charles E. Smith and Ralph Ellison.
ESTRAD. Sweden. 1929–.
ETHNOMUSICOLOGY. U.S.A. 1955–.
EUREKA. U.K. 1960.
GOODCHILD'S JAZZ BULLETIN. U.K. 196?
GRAMOPHONE. U.K. 1923–. Indexed *Music Index.* Leading British musical periodical devoted mainly to classical music and technical problems of sound reproduction, but has an impressive panel of jazz record reviewers and some of the best reviews.
HRS RAG. U.S.A. 1940–1941.
HAAGSE JAZZ CLUB. Netherlands. 1951–.
HIP: the Milwaukee jazz letter. U.S.A. 1963–.
HOT CLUB OF JAPAN BULLETIN. Japan.

HOT NEWS. U.K. 1935–?

HOT NOTES. Ireland, 1946–1948.

INTERNATIONAL DISCOPHILE. U.S.A.

JAZZ. (In Polish.) Poland. 1956–. Poland's only jazz magazine. It is printed, with numerous illustrations, on a rather poor-quality paper. Includes some material on popular artists which is outside the interests of most jazz students. The usual ingredients of features, news, reviews, etc.

JAZZ: a quarterly of American music. U.S.A. 1958–1961.

JAZZ AND POP (formerly *Jazz*). U.S.A. 1962–. In its earlier years was one of the best American magazines. Indexed *Music Index.*

JAZZ BEAT. (Formerly *JAZZ NEWS*) (q.v.) U.K. 1964–1966. Successor to *Jazz News* which lasted as a weekly for some years. This magazine tried to be 'newsy' with bits of gossip, plenty of pictures, short articles, some record reviews and a jazz club guide. It had a more professional look than most jazz magazines.

JAZZ BULLETIN. Switzerland.

JAZZ DI IERE E DI OGGI. (In Italian.) Italy.

JAZZ- DISCO. Sweden. 1960–. Discographical journal.

JAZZ DISCOGRAPHY. 1960–.

JAZZ FAN. U.K. 195–?

JAZZ FORUM. (European Jazz Federation.) (In English and Polish.) Poland. 1968?–.

JAZZ FORUM: quarterly review of jazz and literature. U.K. 1946–1947. Some well-written articles by distinguished contributors. An unusual venture combining literature with jazz.

JAZZ GUIDE. U.K. 1964–.

JAZZ-HOT: la revue internationale du jazz. (In French.) France. 1935–1939, 1945–. Indexed in *Music Index.*

JAZZ ILLUSTRATED. U.K. 1949–? All pictures and current news with a few record reviews for good measure. Little of permanent value.

JAZZ INFORMATION. U.S.A. 1939–1941.

JAZZ JOURNAL. (In Dutch.) Netherlands.

JAZZ JOURNAL. U.K. 1948–. Covers the whole field of jazz in a responsible and adult manner and is indispensable to the jazz student. Many articles of permanent value have appeared in it since its inception and its record reviews are by recognised authorities. Well printed—it also issues an annual index. Indexed *Music Index.*

JAZZ KATALOG. (In German.) Germany. 1959–.

JAZZ MAGAZINE. (In French.) France, 1954–. Nicely printed and artistically produced journal. Similar formula to British *Jazz Journal,* etc. with features, reviews, news and photographs.

JAZZ MAGAZINE. Argentina, 1945–46.

JAZZ MONTHLY. (Incorporated *JAZZ RECORDS: a monthly* discographical listing of current jazz releases 1962–1966.) U.K. 1954–. One of the two leading magazines published in Britain devoted entirely to jazz. Full length articles are usually well written and the record review section is an invaluable guide to the plethora of new jazz releases. There is a regular discographical feature, photographs, letters to the editor and book and periodical reviews.

JAZZ MUSIC: the international jazz magazine (incorporates *Hot News, Discography* and *Jazz Tempo* q.v.). U.K. 1942–1944, 1946–1960. Between 1944 and 1946 ten booklets in the Jazz Music Books series were published in place of the magazine. Most influential of the British magazines published during the war years—a period of great activity.

JAZZ MUSIK. (In German.) Germany.

JAZZ NEWS. U.K. 1956–1964.

JAZZ NOTES. U.S.A.

JAZZ NOTES. Australia, 1940–?

JAZZ ORCHESTRAS. U.K. 1946–? Printed magazine (20 pp.) with articles on various jazz artists. With illustrations.

JAZZ PODIUM. (In German.) Germany 1952–. Circulates in both East and West Germany and Austria and Switzerland. Contains news, features, reviews, etc. Probably the most important jazz magazine in the German language.

JAZZ RECORD. U.K. 1943–1944.

JAZZ REGISTER. U.K. 1965–.

JAZZ REPORT. U.S.A.

JAZZ REPORT. U.S.A. 1958–. Indexed in *Music Index.*

JAZZ REVIEW. U.S.A. 1958–1961. Probably the best jazz periodical produced in the U.S.A. Authoritative, academic and perhaps a little too serious but contributions of a high standard which mean that the $3\frac{1}{2}$ years of the magazine included a great deal of permanent value to the jazz student. Martin Williams selects from these pages in his two anthologies *Art of Jazz* (1959) and *Jazz Panorama* (1962). Indexed in *Music Index.*

JAZZ, RHYTHM AND BLUES. (In English, French and German.) Switzerland. 1967–.

JAZZ SCENE. U.K. 1962–.

JAZZ SHOP: a bi-monthly magazine for collectors. Italy.

JAZZ STATISTICS. Switzerland. 1956–1963. Discographical magazine.

JAZZ STUDIES. U K. 1964–.

JAZZ TEMPO. U.K. 1943–1944.

JAZZ TIMES: Bulletin of the West London Jazz Society. U.K. 1964–. Successor to earlier Steve Lane journals including *Jazz Music* which appeared for 10 years from 1950–1960. Belongs firmly in the 'traditional' school and is mainly of local interest.

JAZZ WERELD: Verschynt elke twee maanden. (In Dutch.) Netherlands, 1965–. Leading Dutch jazz magazine—feature articles, book and record reviews.

JAZZ WRITINGS. U.K. 1936–?

JAZZBLADID. (In Icelandic.) Iceland.

JAZZBRIEF. (In German.) Germany 1960–.

JAZZFINDER. U.S.A. 1948–1949.

JAZZFREUND: Mitterlungs blatt fur Jazzfreunde in Ost und West. (In German.) Germany. 1956–.

JAZZLAND. (In Italian.) Italy.

JAZZOMANIA. Argentina.

JAZZOPATERS INSIDE INFORMATION. (In German.) Germany. 1957–.

JAZZREVY. (In Danish.) Denmark. 1953?–.

JUST JASS. U.K. 1962. Duplicated local news-sheet on the Birmingham jazz scene and thus mainly of local interest to fans in that area.

MATRIX (incorporating *Discophile*) (q.v.) Jazz record research magazine. U.K. 1954–. Duplicated discographical magazine—useful in its specialised field. Indexed in *Music Index.*

MELODY MAKER (incorporates *Rhythm* q.v.). U.K. 1926–. Indexed in *Music Index.*

METRONOME. U.S.A. 1885–1961.

METRONOME YEARBOOK. U.S.A. 1950–1961.

MUSIC: Le magazine du jazz. (In French.) Belgium, 1924–1939.

MUSIC INDEX: a subject-author guide to over 150 current periodicals from the U.S., England, Canada, Australia and 15 non-English language countries. U.S.A. 1949–. Indexes 14–15 of the leading jazz periodicals.

MUSIC MAKER. U.K. 1966–. Not strictly a jazz magazine but a sample issue includes about 50 per cent of interest to the jazz enthusiast. Glossy and well produced with some interesting material.

MUSIC MEMORIES AND JAZZ REPORT: covering all phases of music collection. (Incorporates *Jazz Report* q.v.) U.S.A. 1961–. It is primarily discographical and a vehicle for exchange, buying and selling of jazz records.

MUSICA JAZZ. (In Italian.) Italy. 1945. Indexed in *Music Index.*

MUSICAL EXPRESS. U.K. 1946–1952.

MUSIGRAM. U.S.A. 1963–.

MUSIK REVUE. (In Danish.) Denmark.

NEW MUSICAL EXPRESS. (Formerly *Musical Express* q.v.) U.K. 1952–. Presently contains little or nothing of jazz interest but earlier issues covered the jazz world. Now a 'pop' music magazine.

NEW YORKER. U.S.A. 1925–. Whitney Balliett writes regularly on jazz. Indexed in *Music Index.*

NORSK JAZZ. (In Norwegian.) Norway. 1955–1957.

ORKESTER JOURNALEN: Tidskrift fur jazzmusik. (In Swedish.) Sweden. 1933–. Well-produced journal. One of the longest-lasting jazz magazines and a major influence in the Scandinavian jazz world. Indexed in *Music Index.*

PICK-UP. U.K. 1946–1947.

PLAYBACK: the jazz record magazine. (Incorporated *Jazzfinder* q.v.) U.S.A. 1948–?

PLAYBOY. U.S.A. 1953–. General man's magazine giving occasional coverage to jazz.

R.S.V.P.: the record collectors journal. U.K. 1966–. Lists records for disposal, some of which are of interest to the jazz collector.

R and B MONTHLY. U.K. 196?–1966. Discographical magazine of value in its field although some material included is outside the strictly jazz field.

RAGTIME SOCIETY (PUBLICATION). Canada. 1962–.

RECORD CHANGER. U.S.A. 1942–1955?

RECORD FINDER. U.S.A. 1958–. Duplicated periodical issued by a California jazz record shop. Consists of items for sale and auction from collectors in U.S.A., Canada and Britain.

RECORD RESEARCH: the magazine of record statistics and information. U.S.A. 1955–. Discographical research periodical comprising mainly, but not entirely, jazz material. Includes several articles in addition to the usual pages of discography and lists of records for auction. Indexed in *Music Index.*

RECORDED FOLK MUSIC. U.K. Often includes material of

interest to the jazz and blues lover although not really a jazz magazine.

REVUE DU JAZZ. (In French.) France. 1948–.

RHYTHM. U.K. 1926–1939.

RHYTHM AND BLUES. U.S.A. ?–1965. Printed magazine of only limited interest to the jazz enthusiast. A good deal of its space was given over to non-jazz material and the quality of much of the writing was poor.

RHYTHM AND BLUES PANORAMA: Bulletin périodique du R.N.B. Club. (In French.) Belgium. 1960–.

RHYTHM AND SOUL U.S.A. U.K. 1966–. Fringe interest only—no real jazz material included.

RHYTHME. (In Dutch.) Netherlands.

RITMO Y MELODIA. (In Spanish.) Spain. 1943–.

RYTMI. (In Finnish.) Finland, 1934–.

SATURDAY REVIEW. U.S.A. 1924–. General literary review regularly includes articles of jazz interest.

SECOND LINE. U.S.A. 1948–. Printed magazine published by the New Orleans Jazz Club 'if and when the men and women . . . have time to devote to it'. Short pieces mainly of a 'newsy' nature and mainly of local interest.

SCHLAGZEUG. (In German.) Germany.

SHEFFIELD UNIVERSITY JAZZ CLUB MAGAZINE. U.K. 1966–. Local magazine with some interesting articles but of no particular significance.

SHOUT. (Continues *SOUL MUSIC MONTHLY*) (q.v.) U.K. 1968–. A comprehensive journal covering the field of Negro rhythm and blues music.

SINCOPA Y RITMO. (In Spanish.) Argentina. 194–?

SOUL. Canada. 1965–.

SOUL MUSIC MONTHLY : the world's leading rhythm and blues magazine. U.K. 1967–1968.

SOUND AND FURY. U.S.A.

STORYVILLE. U.K. 1965–. A well-produced journal neatly produced with a mixture of discographical information and general articles. Special trading section paged separately with lists of records for sale (and in no. 3 an excellent guide to the assessment and designation of condition of gramophone records).

SWEET AND HOT MAGAZINE. Belgium. 1960–.

SWING JOURNAL. (In Japanese.) Japan. 1947–.

SWING MUSIC. U.K. 1935–1936.

SWING TIME: Revue mensuelle de la musique de jazz. (In French.) Belgium. 1950–1956.

THEME. U.S.A. 1953–.

VARIETY. U.S.A.

VIBRATIONS: the sound of the jazz community. U.S.A. 1967–.

VINTAGE JAZZ MART. U.K. 19?–. This magazine is purely a vehicle for buying, selling and exchanging jazz records. Circulates internationally and includes much unobtainable material. Extremely difficult to read with the naked eye! Invaluable to the true collector. Absorbed *Jazz Music* (q.v.) several years ago.

CHAPTER 7

JAZZ AND LITERATURE

Since the time in the late 1930's when writing on jazz really got under way there have been links between this musical form and the creative artist. In fact as far as films are concerned, as discussed in the appendix, the connection dates from the invention of talking motion pictures in 1928. Most examples in this chapter are works of fiction with a jazz theme, about a jazz-playing character or set in a jazz environment. Brief references are made to poetry and jazz, and to the one or two plays with a jazz theme.

One of the earliest jazz novels is Dorothy Baker's *Young man with a horn*, which was written eight years after the death of Chicago-style jazz cornet player Leon 'Bix' Beiderbecke and is loosely based on his brief but colourful career. Although by no means a major work of fiction it has some interest and since its original publication in 1938 has reappeared in many editions including book club and paperback up to 1962. In the early 1950's it was filmed (not very successfully) under the title in Britain of *Young man of music* (see also Chapter 8). It should be said here that there are no jazz novels which stand in the first rank of literature and just as the definitive jazz film has yet to be made, they remain to be written. There are a number of books of the second rank which are worthy of attention and which contribute, in some cases, to a better understanding of jazz. There are others which have little literary merit and fail completely to get 'under the skin' of the jazzmen who are their main characters.

John A. Williams, a Negro author, has written *Night Song* (1961) which is perhaps the most believable of all the attempts to make fictional sense of a Negro jazzman's life. British writer Roland Gant's book *World in a jug* (1959) had its share of faults but it did also give a realistic picture of a jazz pianist who lived an unnatural life out of a suitcase. This world of the one-night-stand—travelling long distances each day and performing in a different town each night—is a common factor in the lives of practising jazzmen, as indeed of other entertainers. Other novels refer to this situation and the stresses and strains it produces on those who live this way. Another British writer who is better qualified than most to write this type of book is Benny Green, who gave up playing professionally as a musician to earn his living as a writer. In another chapter there is mentioned some of his jazz criticism but here his *Blame it on my youth* is relevant, even though the actual amount of jazz itself in the book is limited. Many of the authors in this sphere look for authenticity by throwing in mentions of the famous names in jazz together with a liberal use of picturesque terminology. This is often very easily seen through by the real expert and spoils his reading of the novel, even if its story line and literary quality is good. Nat Hentoff, whose work has appeared throughout this book, understands the feelings of Negro musicians extremely well and his *Jazz Country*, which is aimed at a mainly youthful readership, is outstanding. In 1959 the leading monthly *Jazz Journal* reviewed John Clellon Holmes *The horn* and found it the 'best jazz novel to date'. Another book which was written around this time and also got some good reviews in the jazz press was Garson Kanin's *Blow up a storm* (1960). Kanin is a skilful author but the novel is only partially successful as the leading character is not well presented. This book was also made available a year after original publication as a paperback. In the biographies chapter reference was made to Ross Russell's *The sound* which fictionalised the life of leading modern jazz saxophonist Charlie Parker. Another claimant to the title of 'the best novel written on jazz' is Herbert Simmons' *Man walking on eggshells* (1962). This was well-written and received critical acclaim on publication. Other books by American authors include Langston Hughes' *Tambourines to glory* (1959), which is the story of two Negro women gospel singers, Evan Hunter's *Second ending* (1956) and Harold

Flender's *Paris Blues.* The latter explored the relationship between two American jazz musicians (one Negro and one white) living and working in Paris. Their creative work is distracted by the presence of two female tourists who attempt to get them to return to the United States. The film version of this book featured the playing of Louis Armstrong and other jazz musicians and Duke Ellington's fine musical score. John Wain, one of the original 'Angry Young Men' of the British literary scene in the mid-1950's, also attempted, with some success, a jazz novel in *Strike the father dead.* Mary Weik's *The jazz man* (1966) is a brief 42-page fable unusually illustrated by Ann Grifalion's woodcuts.

Few stage plays have had jazz themes but one outstanding exception was *The connection*, which ran in New York before being made into a successful film directed by Shirley Clarke in 1961. The theme tells of a group of heroin addicts who are waiting for their 'connection' to arrive with the drug. The score was written by pianist Freddie Redd and played on stage by him and others, including saxophonist Jackie McLean, in both the stage and film versions. The quality of the music was excellent and in some ways it provides the most serious presentation of jazz in a feature film. Edward Albee's play *Death of Bessie Smith* has links with jazz through its treatment of the racial prejudice which affected the road accident when the famous blues singer met her death.

Jazz and poetry have enjoyed a recent vogue but most of the poetry had no connection in subject content with the music which was played as an accompaniment. Poets like Christopher Logue have been associated with this movement in Britain. Jazz poetry has appeared in various collections though none of major significance. Negro poet Langston Hughes produced an early anthology in 1926 entitled *The weary blues* and other more recent collections include Jake Trussell's *After hours poetry* (1959), Rosey Pool's *Beyond the blues* (1962) and John Sinclair's *This is our music* (1965).

BIBLIOGRAPHY

ALBEE, E. 'The death of Bessie Smith' (*in Zoo story: The death of Bessie Smith and The sandbox:* three plays introduced by the author). New York, Coward-McCann, 1960.
—— —— London, Samuel French, 1968. Acting edition of the play.
ALLEN, S. *Bop fables.* New York, Simon and Schuster, 1955.
AVERY, R. *Murder on the downbeat.* New York, Mystery House, 1943.
BAIRD, J. *Hot, sweet and blue.* New York, Fawcett Publications, 1956.
BAKER, D. *Young man with a horn.* Boston, Houghton Mifflin, 1938.
—— —— London, Victor Gollancz, 1938.
—— —— New York, Readers Club, 1943.
—— —— New York, Dial Press, 1944.
—— —— Cleveland, World Publishing Co., 1946. Paperback edition.
—— —— London, Jazz Book Club, 1957.
—— —— London, Transworld, 1962.
BIRD, B. *Downbeat for a dirge.* New York, Dodd, Mead, 1952.
—— *Dead and gone.* (Paperback ed. of *Downbeat for a dirge.*) New York, Dell, 195?
BORNEMAN, E. *Tremolo.* New York, Harper, 1948.
—— —— London, Jarrolds, 1948.
—— —— London, Four Square Books, 1960. (Published under the title *Something wrong.*)
BROSSARD, C. *Who walk in darkness.* New York, New Directions, 1952.
—— —— London, John Lehmann, 1952.
—— —— New York, Signet, 1954.
CLAPHAM, W. *Come blow your horn.* London, Cape, 1958.
—— —— Toronto, Clarke Irwin, 1958.
CURRAN, D. *Dupree blues.* New York, Knopf, 1948.
—— —— New York, Berkeley, 19? Paperback edition.
—— *Piano in the band.* New York, Reynal and Hitchcock, 1940.
CUTHBERT, C. *The robbed heart.* New York, Fischer, 1945.
—— —— New York, Dell, 19?
DUKE, O. *Sideman.* New York, Criterion, 1956.
ENGLISH, R. *Strictly ding-dong and other swing stories.* Garden City, N.Y., Doubleday, Doran, 1941.
EWING, A. *Little gate.* New York, Rinehart, 1947.

FLENDER, H. *Paris blues.* New York, Ballantine, 1957.
—— —— London, Hamilton & Co., 1961.
FOOTE, S. 'Ride out' (*in* ASWELL, M. L. *New short novels,* New York, Ballantine, 1954. pp. 1–52).
GANT, R. *World in a jug.* London, Cape, 1959.
—— —— New York, Vanguard Press, 1961.
GELBER, J. *The connection: a play.* New York, Grove Press, 1960.
—— —— London, Evergreen Books, 1960.
GILBERT, E. *The hot and the cool.* Garden City, N.Y., Doubleday, 1953.
—— —— New York, Popular Library, 1954. Paperback edition.
GOFFIN, R. *Jazz band.* Bruxelles, Le Disque Vert, 1921. (In French.) Poems.
GREEN, B. *Blame it on my youth.* London, MacGibbon and Kee, 1967.
GWINN, W. *Jazz bum.* New York, Lion Books, 1954.
HANLEY, J. *Hot lips.* New York, Designs Publishing Corporation, 1952.
HARVEY, C. ed. *Jazz parody: anthology of jazz fiction.* London, Spearman, 1948.
HENTOFF, N. *Jazz country.* New York, Harper, 1965.
—— —— London, Hart-Davis, 1966.
HOLMES, J. C. *Go.* New York, Scribners, 1952.
—— *The horn.* New York, Random House, 1958.
—— —— London, Deutsch, 1959.
—— —— London, Jazz Book Club, 1961.
HUGHES, L. *Tambourines to glory, a novel.* New York, J. Day Co., 1958. Story of two Negro women gospel singers.
—— —— London, Gollancz, 1959.
—— *The weary blues: with an introduction by Carl Van Vechten.* New York, Knopf, 1926. Poems.
HUNTER, E. *Second ending.* New York, Simon and Schuster, 1956.
—— —— London, Constable, 1956.
—— —— London, Transworld, 1957. Paperback edition.
JOANS, T. *Jazz poems.* New York, Rhino Review, 1959.
KANIN, G. *Blow up a storm.* New York, Random House, 1959.
—— —— London, Heinemann, 1960.
—— —— London, Hamilton, 1961. Paperback edition.
KELLEY, W. M. *A drop of patience.* New York, Doubleday, 1965.
KEROUAC, J. *On the road.* New York, Viking Press, 1957.
—— —— London, Deutsch, 1958.
—— —— London, Pan Books, 1961.

—— *The subterraneans.* New York, Grove Press, 1958.
—— —— London, A. Deutsch, 1960.
LEA, G. *Somewhere there's music.* Philadelphia, Lippincott, 1958.
LEE, G. W. *Beale Street sundown.* New York, House of Field, 1942.
MILLEN, G. *Sweet man.* London, Cassell, 1930.
—— —— New York, Pyramid, 1952. Paperback edition.
MITCHELL, A. *If you see me comin'.* London, Cape, 1962.
—— —— New York, Macmillan, 1962.
POOL, R. E. comp. *Beyond the blues.* Lympne, Kent, Hand and Flower Press, 1962. Poems by American Negroes.
RIEMAN, T. *Vamp till ready.* New York, Harper, 1954.
—— —— London, Gollancz, 1955.
RUNDELL, W. *Jazz band.* New York, Greenberg, 1935.
RUSSELL, R. *The sound.* New York, Dutton, 1961. Novel based on the life of saxophonist Charlie Parker.
—— —— London, Cassell, 1962.
SHURMAN, I. *Death beats the band.* New York, Phoenix Press, 1943.
SIMMONS, H. A. *Man walking on eggshells.* Boston, Houghton Mifflin, 1962.
—— —— London, Methuen, 1962.
—— —— London, Jazz Book Club, 1964.
SIMON, G. T. *Don Watson starts his band*; foreword by Benny Goodman. New York, Dodd Mead, 1940. (For children.)
SINCLAIR, H. *Music out of Dixie.* New York, Rinehart, 1952.
—— —— New York, Permabooks, 1953.
SINCLAIR, J. *This is our music.* Detroit, Artists Workshop Press, 1965. Poems.
SKLAR, G. *The two worlds of Johnny Truro.* Boston, Little, Brown, 1947.
—— —— Reprint ed. Garden City, N.Y., Sun Dial Press, 1948.
—— —— (Special abridged edition.) New York, Popular Library, 1950.
SMITH, R. P. *So it doesn't whistle.* New York, Harcourt Brace, 1941.
—— *Plus blood in their veins.* New York, Avon, 1952. (Paperback edition of *So it doesn't whistle.*)
SPICER, B. *Blues for the prince.* New York, Dodd, Mead, 1950.
—— —— London, Collins 1951.
—— —— New York, Bantam Books, 1951.
STEIG, H. *Send me down.* New York, Knopf, 1941.
—— —— New York, Avon, 19?

—— —— London, Jarrolds, 1943.
STEPHENS, E. *Roman joy.* New York, Doubleday, 1965.
SYLVESTER, R. *Rough sketch.* New York, Dial Press, 1948.
TRUSSELL, J. *After hours poetry.* Kingsville, Texas, The author, 1958.
UPDYKE, J. *It's always four o'clock.* New York, Random House, 1956.
VAN VECHTEN, C. *Nigger heaven.* New York, Knopf, 1926.
—— —— London, Knopf, 1926.
—— —— New York, Avon, n.d.
WAIN, J. *Strike the father dead.* London, Macmillan, 1962.
WALLOP, D. *Night light.* New York, Norton, 1953.
WEIK, M. H. *The jazz man.* New York, Atheneum, 1966. Children's fable illustrated by woodcuts by Ann Grifalion.
WHITMORE, S. *Solo.* New York, Harcourt Brace, 1955.
—— —— London, Gollancz, 1956.
—— —— London, Transworld, 1958. Paperback edition.
WILLIAMS, J. *Night song.* New York, Farrar, Straus and Giroux, 1961.
—— —— London, Collins, 1962.
—— —— London, Jazz Book Club, 196?
WILLIS, G. *Little boy blues.* New York, Dutton, 1947.
—— *Tangleweed.* Garden City, New York, Doubleday, Doran & Co., 1943.
—— *The wild faun.* New York, Greenberg, 1945.

CHAPTER 8

ORGANISATIONS

Jazz has been poorly served until very recent times by specialist organisations. Those bodies which have been formed have been transient, somewhat factional and lacking in adequate funds. The basis for a longer-term success is extremely difficult to provide and the publicly supported bodies such as government (both national and local) and educational institutions (such as colleges and universities) have been slow indeed to step in.

The effort of individuals to persuade these reluctant sponsors has been praiseworthy but has conspicuously lacked mass support. Jazz supporters appear to have been slow to realise the need to collect historical data of all kinds. Professor Marshall Stearns, whose historical writings on jazz have been noted in an earlier chapter, was the prime mover in setting up the Institute of Jazz Studies in New York in 1952. The Institute has since moved to Rutgers University, New Jersey, where its future should be assured. Its stated aims are 'to give jazz the serious study and attention it deserves and to foster an understanding and appreciation of the nature and significance of jazz in our society'. In following these aims the Institute has subsequently developed into the world's top research centre on the subject and has built up a substantial document collection as well as a record collection and items of museum interest. Queries on all aspects of jazz are received from many parts of the world.

Other organisations of either direct or marginal interest to the jazz student in the United States include the Archive of American Folk-Song based at the Library of Congress in Washington. This Archive includes some 75,000 folksongs and stories on 17,500 recordings and was established in

1928. It was a pioneer project in the documentary recording of the folk traditions of the United States. It is the leading repository for American folk music recordings, as well as being an important archive for folk music from all over the world. It recently received a research grant to investigate the feasibility of a computer-produced catalogue. An article on the work of the Archive appeared in *Blues Unlimited* in April 1965.

Organisations based on the New Orleans area are the New Orleans Jazz Museum and the Archive of New Orleans Jazz at Tulane University. The former was established in 1959 and has a collection of old musical instruments used by famous jazz musicians, records and tapes, sheet music, jazz posters, contracts and photographs together with a library. The bulk of the collection in the Archive at Tulane (established one year earlier) consists of taped interviews with New Orleans musicians. Other holdings include records, sheet music, photographs, posters and clippings, as well as the special La Rocca collection of documents on the Original Dixieland Jazz Band. Recent references to the work of the Archive appeared in *Coda,* and in the *Wilson Library Bulletin,* and progress reports on the Museum appear regularly in *The Second Line,* the magazine of the New Orleans Jazz Club.

In the Louisiana division of the New Orleans Public Library there is a collection of jazz literature together with a comprehensive file collection of pictures, clippings, magazine articles and programmes. In the Art and Music Department of the Library there is the Souchon Jazz and Folk Music Collection which consists primarily of recordings (over 2,000 items) pertaining to the history of early New Orleans jazz. A few recordings of the music of Africa and the Caribbean, together with a small number of documents, complete the collection. It was presented to the Library in the early 1950's by Dr. Edmond Souchon, a leading New Orleans supporter of jazz music. After being catalogued and arranged by Richard Allen, it was officially opened for reference use in May 1952. A contemporary newspaper article described the scope of the collection in the following words: 'In addition to the local material, countries represented include Africa, Haiti, Mexico, Venezuela, Brazil, Java, Sumatra, Bali and Malaya. The collection represents Dr. Souchon's interest in tracing the evolution of jazz from its folk origins to its birth in New Orleans and through its subsequent development as a world-wide art form. . . . Some of the items of particular interest in the collection which library officials say will be the largest public jazz collection in the nation, are the Library of Congress series of folk music, the Alan Lomax interviews with Jelly Roll Morton in 12 albums, and the records of local musicians and bands.' The collection is available for serious research only and is not classified.

A fringe society which is of some interest is the National Sheet Music Society Inc., which is a non-profit making organisation serving collectors and students of American printed music. Its regular journal *Musigram* issued nine times a year often includes articles of jazz interest and other items on American folk music which are of interest to the student. Sample titles of articles which have appeared are 'Origin of Negro Spirituals', 'Ragtime pioneers in Sedalia' and 'An explanation of jazz'. The society has members throughout the U.S.A. and Canada and exists 'to learn more about American sheet music, songs, tunes, composers and performers etc.'

In Britain a pioneer organisation was the National Federation of Jazz Organisations which existed for a few years from about 1948 to 1953. This was an umbrella organisation for the many new jazz clubs of that period and the main aim of it and its successor, the National Jazz Federation, appeared to be to promote 'live' jazz in the United Kingdom via the concert hall and the jazz club.

Of more recent date is the foundation in 1964 of the British Institute of Jazz Studies which consists of a small but dedicated band of enthusiasts trying to promote the interests of jazz in various ways including the provision of library and information services. This group issue a regular monthly *Newsletter* as well as a quarterly *Jazz Studies.*

The Contemporary Jazz Association founded in 1965 has stated its aims as:

1. to publish a regular newsletter,
2. to establish clubs,
3. to try and establish a direction for British jazz and
   stimulate concerts of new British jazz compositions.

This last aim seems to be perhaps the most important of
the three. A reference to this Association appeared in *Jazz
Monthly* in 1965. A highly specialised group is the Promotional Society for New Orleans Music which is described in
Jazz Times for September 1964.

A completely different body which did much to promote
interest in the jazz literature particularly was the Jazz Book
Club which lasted for eleven years from 1956–1967. Over 70
reasonably priced titles were offered during its existence
and most of the important jazz books appeared over its
imprint. For most of its existence a regular magazine for
members was published entitled *Jazz Column.*

Jazz books are often handled by the specialised record
shops and it is easier to obtain them through this channel
than through the general bookshop. In Britain only one
shop is listed in the appropriate reference guides as
specialising in jazz literature—this is the Bloomsbury
Bookshop of Teresa Chilton which is located in Great
Ormonde Street in London.

Jazz organisations also exist in other countries but
mention will be made only of the Netherlands where co-
operation between the Stichting Jazz in Nederland (Netherlands Jazz Institute) and the Stichting Algemene Openbare
Bibliotheek Nijmegen (Nijmegen Public Library) shows
what can be achieved in this way. A radio interview to
publicise the need for a national collection on jazz by Arie
Elings, the library's director, produced over 1,000 volumes
to make a start. Once the 2,000 volume figure is passed, the
library is then entitled to state-aid to maintain it. This is an
exciting and stimulating development and it would be
interesting indeed to see it pursued elsewhere.

BIBLIOGRAPHY

ALLEN, R. B. New Orleans Jazz Archive at Tulane, *Wilson Library Bulletin,* Mar. 1966, pp. 619, 621–623.

ARCHIVE of American Folk-song, *Blues Unlimited,* Apr. 1965, pp. 3–5.

COLLIER, G. Contemporary Jazz Association. *Jazz Monthly,* v. 11 (10), 1965, p. 30. Letter describing the aims of the Association.

HARRIS, S. The Institute of Jazz Studies. *Jazz Journal* v. 16 (6), 1963, pp. 23–24. Describes the services offered by the Institute.

PROMOTIONAL Society for New Orleans music. *Jazz Times,* Sept. 1964, pp. 4–5.

SPIVACKE, H. A national archive of sound recordings. *Library Journal,* v. 88 (18), 1963, pp. 3783–3788. Includes a mention of the Archive of American Folksong.

(WITHERDEN, B. A.) The European Jazz Federation. *Jazz Studies,* vol. 2(1), Jan. 1968, p. 17. Describes the inaugural meetings and aims of the international organisation which includes the following countries: Austria, Belgium, Czechoslovakia, Finland, East Germany, West Germany, Poland, Italy, Hungary, Yugoslavia and Great Britain.

LIST OF ORGANISATIONS

ARCHIVE OF AMERICAN FOLK-SONG. Library of Congress, Washington, D.C., U.S.A. Established 1928.

ARCHIVE OF NEW ORLEANS JAZZ. Tulane University, New Orleans, La., U.S.A. Established 1958. Curator: Richard B. Allen.

BLOOMSBURY BOOKSHOP. 31–35 Great Ormonde Street, London. Proprietor: Teresa Chilton.

BRITISH INSTITUTE OF JAZZ STUDIES. 14 Beech Road, Pear Tree Acres, Chinnor, Oxon, U.K. Established 1964. Secretary: Michael A. Wood. Publications: 1. *Jazz studies,* Quarterly, 1964–. 2. *B.I.J.S. Newsletter,* Monthly, 1966–.

CONTEMPORARY JAZZ ASSOCIATION. London, U.K. Established 1965. Directors: Graham Collier, Peter Conton and Neil Ardley.

INSTITUTE OF JAZZ STUDIES. Rutgers University, New Brunswick, N.J. 08903, U.S.A. Established 1952. Curator: Charles A. Nanry.

JAZZ BOOK CLUB (now defunct). 10–13 Bedford Street, London, W.C.2, U.K. Established 1956. Finished 1967. Publication *Jazz Column* Bi-monthly 1957–1967.

NATIONAL FEDERATION OF JAZZ ORGANISATIONS (now defunct). London, U.K. 1949–1953?

NATIONAL JAZZ FEDERATION. London, U.K. 1954?–

NATIONAL SHEET MUSIC SOCIETY INC. 5010, Reeder Aven, Covina, Calif. 91723, U.S.A. President: Clarence H. Hogue. Publication *Musigram* 9 per annum 1963–.

NEW ORLEANS JAZZ MUSEUM. 1017 Du Maine Street, New Orleans, La., U.S.A. Established 1959. Curator: Clay Watson.

NEW ORLEANS PUBLIC LIBRARY. 219 Loyola Avenue, New Orleans, La. 70140, U.S.A. *Includes* Souchon Jazz and Folk Music Collection.

PROMOTIONAL SOCIETY FOR NEW ORLEANS MUSIC. London, U.K. President: Barry Martyn.

STICHTING JAZZ IN NEDERLAND (Netherlands Jazz Institute). Oaertroom 536, Amsterdam W, Netherlands. Chairman: Ben Bunders.

APPENDIX

JAZZ ON FILM

The best critical discussion of jazz and the film is by Dan Morgenstern in the *Downbeat yearbook 1966*. In his opening paragraph he points out that jazz and the cinema are 'the two arts truly indigenous to our time'. They have a great deal in common including humble and obscure origins in the later years of the nineteenth century and belated recognition as legitimate forms of artistic expression. The ironic fact is that although it would seem, therefore, that ideal conditions existed for mutual inspiration there is little real achievement to be recorded. The Original Dixieland Jazz Band appeared soundless in the 1917 film *Good for nothing*, filmed at Reisenweber's Restaurant in New York and thus recorded another 'first' performance parallel-ing their first gramophone record. It was with the coming of sound movies in 1928 that the musicians were able to make an impact and over the 40 years to date they have appeared in many films and have composed and performed background music for many others. Unfortunately not a single jazz film—fictional or documentary—that could be called a masterpiece has yet been made. There have been some praiseworthy efforts however, dating back to director Dudley Murphy's *St. Louis blues* and *Black and tan fantasy*, which were both made in 1929. In many of the cases the mere preservation of some of the incomparable jazz artists of the 1920's and 1930's is sufficient to make them of real value to the jazz historian.

The Vitaphone company pioneered the jazz 'short' which was often made for the Negro market and also as 'fillers' for cinema programmes. These films were often extremely com-mercial with banal story lines but, in spite of this, they show many musicians in the prime of their playing careers. The *St. Louis blues* mentioned above featured the empress of all the blues singers, Bessie Smith, and was the only film appearance she ever made. Morgenstern, in his article, comments on her tremendous presence and suggests that she would have made a great actress given the chance. The film is brief—only ten minutes—and the theme simple but its impact is considerable. It also features a band led by pianist James P. Johnson and the Hall Johnson Choir. The other film made by Murphy around the same time features the Duke Ellington orchestra and thus starts a long association as far as Ellington and the film world are concerned. It provides an opportunity to see and hear the orchestra in its earliest days and it is particularly interesting to see such musicians as Johnny Hodges, Harry Carney and Cootie Williams who are still with Ellington forty years later.

The pattern of relationships between jazz and the film developed over the years and the following broad categories can be defined—

(a) commercial shorts;
(b) the use of jazz musicians in cameo performances within the basic framework of film musicals;
(c) the dramatic feature film with a jazz theme including 'biographies' of famous musicians;
(d) the jazz documentary presenting its subject in a straightforward or possibly, arty way;
(e) the all-Negro film—either all-star aimed at the general market or made exclusively for the 'race' market;
(f) the films using jazz music and musicians as background score with little or no jazz aspects in their subject content. Also the impressionist colour films can be included in this category.

The first category—commercial short subjects—were produced mainly in the 1930's and 1940's and many leading bands of that period made at least one. Examples are *Big name bands* (1941 and 1945), *Fats Waller no. 1* and particularly *Rhapsody in black and blue* (1930), which featured Armstrong on the threshold of world fame and at the height of his powers. Armstrong's only other appearance in a film of this type was in *I'll be glad when you're dead, you rascal you* (1930). This was a surrealistic cartoon by Max Fleischer. Duke Ellington also made some interesting 'shorts' in the early 1930's. The first was *Bundle of blues* (1933) and the second *Symphony in black* (1935) received an Oscar nomination. For the connoisseur, however, the most notable feature of the picture was a brief appearance by the young Billie Holiday.

The second category—the cameo spots in musicals—is longer living than the previous one. From the early 1930's to the present day this has been a favourite approach by the film makers. Again Ellington and Armstrong have had their share of activity. Indeed the latter's acting abilities were so obvious that in some films (*Pennies from heaven,* 1936 was an early example) he had a dual role. Count Basie, Goodman, Bechet, Cab Calloway, Jack Teagarden, Ella Fitzgerald and many others have also been involved with this group of films. These seem to be relatively marginal and are not discussed in detail here.

The third category of dramatic features is perhaps mainly notable for its general inaccurate and careless approach. The biographies—*The Benny Goodman Story* (1955), *The Glenn Miller Story* (1954), *The Gene Krupa Story* (195?), *The Five Pennies* (1959) (Red Nichols Story), *The St. Louis blues* (1958) (W. C. Handy) and *The fabulous Dorseys* (1947)—are all fictionalised to such a degree that their historical value is dubious. *The fabulous Dorseys* is probably the best of the bunch mainly because the Dorseys played themselves. Some of the films did, however, contain moments of good jazz. *New Orleans* (1947) had a trite storyline but had some good musical moments too, involving Armstrong and an excellent small group including Kid Ory, Barney Bigard, Zutty Singleton and others. Billie Holiday had a role in the film and her singing is perhaps the best thing in the picture. Woody Herman also appears with his orchestra. *Paris blues* (1960), which was mentioned in the previous chapter, is one of the best attempts to get the atmosphere of a working jazz musician's life and both the acting and musical side were well above average for the jazz film.

The jazz documentary has, on the whole, been much more successful although in some cases a tendency to over-emphasise the visual effects has been detrimental. No survey of the jazz film could avoid a reference to Bert Stern's *Jazz on a summer's day* (1959) which was shot at the 1958 Newport Jazz Festival. Its jazz content is uneven in quality but none the less varied and undiluted. The film was widely distributed and is undoubtedly a milestone in jazz-film history. Again Armstrong appears with Guiffre, Mahalia Jackson and Anita O'Day among others. Another excellent documentary is *Big Bill's blues* made by Belgian Yannick Bruynoghe. This includes the music of blues-singer Broonzy as well as biographical commentary. A television film on Louis Armstrong, with a narration by Edward R. Morrow, was *Satchmo the great* (1956). This includes Armstrong reminiscing on his New Orleans days, and he is seen on tour in Europe, America and, most interesting of all, Africa. British director Jack Gold made a 40-minute television film on the Bruce Turner band, showing its experiences on the touring circuit. This was *Living jazz* (1961)—an interesting film. Many critics agree that one of the best jazz films ever made was *Jammin' the blues* (1944). This features Lester Young and was superbly directed by Gjon Mili. The film is remarkably photographed with an excellent merging of the visual and the aural. The all-Negro film was pioneered by King Vidor with *Hallelujah* (1929) which contained plenty of spirituals and gospel singing but no jazz. There was some blues-singing by Victoria Spivey. *Stormy Weather* (1942) had more jazz emphasis and featured Lena Horne, Cab Calloway and best of all 'Fats' Waller. The next year *Cabin in the sky* appeared with Ethel Waters, Louis Armstrong (acting and playing) and Duke Ellington.

The final category for discussion is the 'jazz as background music' group. Some of these scores have been outstanding and it is an interesting fact that many of the best scores by United States musicians have been for foreign films. An excellent example is the French *Lift to the scaffold* (1962) with a superb score by Miles Davis and played by him and a quartet of French and American musicians. An article on this film appeared in *Jazz Monthly*, Feb. 1962, v. 7 (12), p. 4–5. John Lewis has also composed two splendid scores for *No sun in Venice* (1957) and *Odds against tomorrow* (1959). British films of this type include *Alfie* (1966) with music by saxophonist Sonny Rollins and two scores by John Dankworth for Joseph Losey's *The Criminal* (1960) and *Sapphire* (1959). Finally it seems appropriate to mention here the short impressionist colour films made in Holland (featuring the Modern Jazz Quartet) and in Canada by Norman McLaren featuring piano jazz in different styles by Oscar Peterson (*Begone dull care* (1949)) and Albert Ammons (*Boogie doodle* (1943)).

A detailed and accurate listing of jazz in the film does not yet exist but scattered information is available from various sources. Apart from Morgenstern's brief critical guide quoted earlier, some useful work has been done by the British Film Institute. That body's education officer, Paddy Whannel, compiled a selected list of 19 feature films and 43 'shorts' in 1966. This is entitled *Jazz on film* and is a very personal selection, as Mr. Whannel states in his preface. Each entry has a brief annotation, giving the jazz musicians featured as well as director, country of origin, date and running time.

Jazz and the cinema have thus had a chequered development. Commercial considerations have almost always intervened and prevented the sympathetic and informed presentation needed to get the best out of the collaboration between these two contemporary and fascinating art forms.

BIBLIOGRAPHY

GAUTIER, H. *Jazz au cinema.* Lyon, Societe d'Etudes de Recherches et de Documentation cinematographiques, 196? (In French.)

HOPE, A. 'Blues in the stalls', *Jazz Monthly, v.* 12 (7), 1966, pp. 2–3. A brief, but useful, survey of jazz on film.

JAMES, M. 'Lift to the scaffold', *Jazz Monthly,* v. 7 (12), 1962, pp. 4–5. Film review.

MORGENSTERN, D. 'Jazz on film' (*in DOWNBEAT Yearbook* 1966, pp. 64–69, 88–91). Useful and wide-ranging survey on the links between jazz and the cinema.

WHANNEL, P. *comp. Jazz on film: a select list of films on jazz.* London, British Film Institute, 1966.

JAZZ FILMS
(The items asterisked are those with jazz scores)

ADVENTURES OF AN ASTERISK. U.S.A. 1957. Lionel Hampton and Benny Carter.

*ALFIE. U.K. 1966. Sonny Rollins.

ALL NIGHT LONG. U.K. 1962. John Dankworth, Charles Mingus and Dave Brubeck. Modernised film version of 'Othello'.

AMAZING BUD POWELL. France. 1963. Bud Powell.

*ANATOMY OF A MURDER. U.S.A. 1959. Duke Ellington.

*ASCENSEUR POUR L'ECHAFAUD. France. 1957. Miles Davis. (English title: *Lift to the scaffold.*)

*ASPHALT JUNGLE. U.S.A. 1950. Duke Ellington.

*AUTUMN SPECTRUM. Netherlands. 1958. Modern Jazz Quartet.

BANDWAGON. U.K. 195? Cy Laurie Band.

BARBER SHOP BLUES. U.S.A. 193?

*BEGONE DULL CARE. Canada. 1949. Oscar Peterson Trio.

BEN POLLACK BAND. U.S.A. 1928. Ben Pollack Band.

BENNY GOODMAN STORY. U.S.A. 1955. Benny Goodman Orchestra.

BIG BILL'S BLUES. Belgium? 196? Big Bill Broonzy.

BIG NAME BANDS NO. 1. U.S.A. 1941. Count Basie and Louis Armstrong.

BIG NAME BANDS NO. 2. U.S.A. 1945. Duke Ellington and Wingy Manone.

BIRTH OF THE BLUES. U.S.A. 1941. Jack Teagarden.

BLACK AND TAN FANTASY. U.S.A. 1929. Duke Ellington.

BOBBY HACKETT AND HIS BAND. U.S.A. 1961. Bobby Hackett.

*BOOGIE DOODLE. Canada. 1948. Albert Ammons.

BUNDLE OF BLUES. U.S.A. 1933. Duke Ellington.

BURGUNDY STREET BLUES. U.S.A. 1934.

CABIN IN THE SKY. U.S.A. 1942. Ethel Waters, Louis Armstrong and Duke Ellington.

CHECK AND DOUBLE CHECK. U.S.A. 1930.

CHRIS BARBER AT THE RICHMOND JAZZ FESTIVAL. U.K. 1962. Chris Barber.

CHRIS BARBER BANDSTAND. U.K. 1962. Chris Barber.

The CONNECTION. U.S.A. 1961. Freddie Redd, Jackie McLean. Based on the play by Jack Gelber (see Chapter 7).

COUNT BASIE AND HIS ORCHESTRA. U.S.A. 19? Count Basie.

*The CRIMINAL. U.K. 1960. John Dankworth, Cleo Laine.

CROSSFIRE. U.S.A. 1947. Kid Ory.

CRY OF JAZZ. U.S.A. 1959. Examines differences between Negro and white Americans in background, temperament and experience and explains why the musical structure of jazz provides an interpretation of Negro life.

DISC JOCKEY JAMBOREE. U.S.A. 1957. Tommy Dorsey, George Shearing and Count Basie.

DJANGO REINHARDT. France. 1958. Django Reinhardt.

DON REDMAN ORCHESTRA. U.S.A. 1934. Don Redman.

DUKE ELLINGTON AND HIS ORCHESTRA. U.S.A. 1961. Duke Ellington.

FABULOUS DORSEYS. U.S.A. 1947. Tommy Dorsey and Jimmy Dorsey.

FATS WALLER NO. 1. U.S.A. 1941. Fats Waller.

*Des FEMMES DISPARAISSENT. France. 19? Art Blakey. (English title: *Disappearing women.*)

FIVE PENNIES. U.S.A. 1959. Louis Armstrong and Red Nichols.

FORM OF JAZZ. U.S.A. 1958.

FOUR HITS AND A MISTER. U.K. 196? Acker Bilk.

GENE KRUPA STORY. U.S.A. 195? Gene Krupa.

GLENN MILLER STORY. U.S.A. 1954. Glenn Miller Orchestra.

GOOD FOR NOTHING. U.S.A. 1917. Original Dixieland Jazz

Band. Silent film which includes the first appearance of a jazz band on the screen.

GYROMORPHOSIS. Netherlands. 1958. Modern Jazz Quartet.

HALLELUJAH. U.S.A. 1929.

HARLEM JAZZ FESTIVAL. U.S.A. 1955. Nat Cole, Count Basie and Sarah Vaughan.

HARLEM ROCK AND ROLL. U.S.A. 1955. Duke Ellington, Lionel Hampton, Nat Cole and Joe Turner.

HARLEM WEDNESDAY. U.S.A. 1958. Benny Carter.

HELLZAPOPPIN. U.S.A. 1941. Slam Stewart, Rex Stewart.

HIGH SOCIETY. U.S.A. 1956. Louis Armstrong.

HOLIDAY. U.K. 195? Chris Barber.

HOLLYWOOD HOTEL. U.S.A. 1938. Benny Goodman.

I WANT TO LIVE. U.S.A. 1958. Gerry Mulligan, Art Farmer and Shelly Manne.

I'LL BE GLAD WHEN YOU'RE DEAD YOU RASCAL YOU. U.S.A. 193? Louis Armstrong.

INTRODUCTION TO JAZZ. U.S.A. 1952. Jellyroll Morton and others.

JAMMIN' THE BLUES. U.S.A. 1944. Lester Young, Illinois Jacquet, Harry Edison, Jo Jones, Sid Catlett, Barney Kessel, Red Callender and Marie Bryant.

JAZZ BALL. U.S.A. 195? Duke Ellington, Artie Shaw, Louis Armstrong, Bing Crosby, Red Nichols and Louis Prima.

JAZZ BANDITEN. Germany. 1959.

JAZZ DANCE. U.S.A. 1954. Willie Smith, Jimmy Archey, Jimmy McPartland, Pee Wee Russell, Pops Foster and George Wettling.

JAZZ FESTIVAL. U.S.A. 1956. Lionel Hampton, Duke Ellington, Stan Kenton and Nat Cole.

JAZZ FOR SMALL BANDS. U.K. 19?

JAZZ FROM '61. U.S.A. 1959. Ahmed Jamal and Ben Webster.

JAZZ ON A SUMMER'S DAY. U.S.A. 1959. Louis Armstrong, Jimmy Guiffre, Mahalia Jackson, Anita O'Day and many others.

LEAVE IT TO HARRY. U.S.A. 1954. Harry James.

Les LIAISONS DANGEREUSE. France. 1959. Duke Jordan, Art Blakey, Thelonius Monk.

LIONEL HAMPTON AND HERB JEFFRIES. U.S.A. 1955. Lionel Hampton and Herb Jeffries.

LIONEL HAMPTON AND HIS ORCHESTRA. U.S.A. 1959.

LIVING JAZZ. U.K. 1961. Bruce Turner.

LOST IN A HAREM. U.S.A. 1944. Jimmy Dorsey's Orchestra.

LOUIS ARMSTRONG AND HIS ORCHESTRA. U.S.A. 19? Louis Armstrong, Earl Hines, Jack Teagarden, Barney Bigard and Sid Catlett.

MCKINNEY'S COTTON PICKERS. U.S.A. 1928. McKinney's Cotton Pickers.

MAN CALLED ADAM. U.S.A. 1965.

*MAN WITH THE GOLDEN ARM. U.S.A. 1956. Elmer Bernstein, Shorty Rogers, Shelly Manne.

MANN WITH THE FLUTE. U.S.A. 19? Herbie Mann.

MARCH OF TIME. U.S.A. 1937. Original Dixieland Jazz Band.

MOMMA DON'T ALLOW. U.K. 1955. Chris Barber.

MOUND CITY BLUE BLOWERS. U.S.A. 1928. Mound City Blue Blowers.

MUSIC IN AMERICA. U.S.A. 1944. Art Tatum, Dave Tough, Eddie Condon, Benny Goodman.

*NEW KIND OF LOVE. U.S.A. 1963. Erroll Garner.

NEW ORLEANS. U.S.A. 1947. Louis Armstrong, Billie Holiday, Woody Herman and others.

NEW ORLEANS FUNERAL. U.S.A. 1962. Bunk Johnson.

*ODDS AGAINST TOMORROW. U.S.A. 1959. John Lewis.

ORCHESTRA WIVES. U.S.A. 1942. Glenn Miller.

PARIS BLUES. U.S.A. 1961. Duke Ellington, Louis Armstrong, Paul Gonsalves.

PENNIES FROM HEAVEN. U.S.A. 1936. Louis Armstrong.

PETE KELLY'S BLUES. U.S.A. 1955. Ella Fitzgerald.

RED NICHOLS AND THE FIVE PENNIES. U.S.A. 1951. Red Nichols.

REPULSION. U.S.A. 19? Chico Hamilton.

REVEILLE WITH BEVERLEY. U.S.A. Duke Ellington, Count Basie.

RHAPSODY IN BLACK AND BLUE. U.S.A. 1930. Louis Armstrong.

RHYTHM ON THE RIVER. U.S.A. 1940. Wingy Manone.

ST. LOUIS BLUES. U.S.A. 1929. Bessie Smith, James P. Johnson.

ST. LOUIS BLUES. U.S.A. 1958. Nat Cole, Mahalia Jackson and others.

*SAIT-ON JAMAIS. France. 1957. John Lewis. (English title: *No sun in Venice.*)

SAPPHIRE. Britain. 1959. John Dankworth.

SATCHMO THE GREAT. U.S.A. 1957. Louis Armstrong.

*SHADOWS. U.S.A. 1961. Charles Mingus.

SHAKE, RATTLE AND ROCK. U.S.A. 1956. Fats Domino and Joe Turner.

666. U.S.A. 1959. Teo Macero.

SMALL BAND JAZZ. U.K. 196? Tony Kinsey.

SONG IS BORN. U.S.A. 1948. Benny Goodman, Louis Armstrong and others.

STEPHANE GRAPPELLY. U.K. 19?

STORMY WEATHER. U.S.A. 1943. Fats Waller, Lena Horne, Cab Calloway.

SUBTERRANEANS. U.S.A. 1960. Gerry Mulligan and Art Farmer.

SUDDENLY ITS JAZZ. Britain. 1963. Dick Charlesworth.

*SWEET SMELL OF SUCCESS. U.S.A. 1957. Chico Hamilton.

SYMPHONY IN BLACK. U.S.A. 1935. Duke Ellington.

SYNCOPATION. U.S.A. 1942. Bunny Berigan, Benny Goodman, Gene Krupa and Harry James.

TAILGATE MAN FROM NEW ORLEANS. France. 1952. Kid Ory.

*Un TEMOIN DANS LA VILLE. France. 19? Kenny Dorham. (English title: *Witness in the city.*)

TENDER GAME. U.S.A. 1958. Oscar Peterson.

TOO LATE BLUES. U.S.A. 1961. Shelly Manne, Benny Carter, Jimmy Rowles, Red Mitchell.

TWILIGHT ON THE PRAIRIE. U.S.A. 1944. Jack Teagarden.

WALKING HILLS. U.S.A. 1949.

*WILD ONE. U.S.A. 1953. Shorty Rogers, Leith Stevens.

YOUNG MAN WITH A HORN. U.S.A. 1950. Harry James, Lionel Hampton. (Entitled *Young man of music* in U.K.)

TITLE INDEX

This index includes titles of books, films and periodicals. The symbol (f) is used to designate a film title and the symbol (p) to denote a periodical title. Where there are two or more entries with the same title, the difference is shown by means of (a) a bracketed author's name for books, e.g. Big bands (Edwards) and Big bands (Simon), (b) a bracketed date for films, e.g. *St. Louis Blues* (1929) and *St. Louis Blues* (1958) and (c) a bracketed country of origin for periodicals, e.g. *Jazz (Poland)* and *Jazz* (U.S.A.).

GENERAL INDEX

Includes both subject and name entries, including authors.

Stewart, Rex, 123
Stewart, Slam, 123
Stichting Algemene Openbare Biblio-
  theek Nijmegen, 114
Stichting Jazz in Nederland, 114, 116
Stock, Dennis, 68, 90
Street bands, 19
Stuart, Jay Alison, *pseud,* 44
Sugrue, Thomas, 41
Sumatra, 113
Swing period, 23–24, 26, 30, 36–37
Swingle, John, 41
Sylvester, Robert, 110

Tait, Dorothy see Stuart, Jay Alison,
  pseud
Tanner, Peter xiii
Tatum, Art, 56, 61,124
Taylor, Cecil, 27, 54, 63
Teagarden, Jack, 27, 36, 47, 64, 70, 90,
  119, 122, 125
Tenot, F., 67, 90
Terkel, Studs, 39
Terminology, 35, 55, 67–68, 85
Testoni, Gian Carlo, 67, 90
Third stream music, 23
Toledano, Ralph de See De Toledano,
  Ralph
Tone colours (in jazz), 1
Tough, Dave, 124
Tracy, Jack, 55, 59
Traditional school of jazz, 22, 28, 35
Traill, Sinclair, 52, 55, 63–64
Tristano, Lennie, 26
Trussell, Jake, 106, 110
Tudor, James, xiv
Tulane University, 112, 115
Turner, Bruce, 123
Turner, Joe, 123, 125
Turner, W. J., 92

Ulanov, Barry, 22, 30, 33, 42, 43, 52, 64
University Microfilms, 71
University theses, 49
Updyke, John, 110
Uptown musicians. (New Orleans), 66

Van Vechten Carl, 108, 110
Vandervoort, Paul, 45
Vaughan, Sarah, 64, 123
Vechten, Carl Van, See Van Vechten,
  Carl
Venables, Ralph, 58, 62, 72
Venezuela, 113
Venuti, Joe, 70
Vidor, King, 120
Vitaphone company, 117

Vogue Records Ltd., 83
Von Haupt, Lois, 49, 64

Wain, John, 106, 110
Walker, Leo, 23, 30
Waller, Thomas 'Fats', 27, 36, 47, 83,
  118, 120, 122, 125
Wallop, Douglass, 110
Ware, C. P., 11
Wareing, C. H., 36, 40
Waterman, Guy, 8, 18, 24, 28
Waters, Ethel, 38, 47, 120, 122
Waters, Howard J., 77, 90
Watson, Clay, 116
Watson, T., 88
Watters, Lu, 52
Weaver, Sylvester, 68
Webster, Ben, 123
Weik, Mary H., 106, 110
West Africa, 1, 3
West Coast jazz, 52
West London Jazz Society, 100
Wettling, George, 123
Whannel, Paddy, 13, 120, 121
White, Josh, 17
White, N. L., 18
Whiteman, Paul, 23, 28, 32, 47
Whitmore, Stanford, 110
Wiedemann, Erik, 67, 86
Wilbraham, Roy, 90
Williams, Anne S, 62
Williams, Cootie, 118
Williams, John A., 104, 110
Williams, Martin T., 8, 18, 24, 26, 27, 28,
  30, 34, 45, 46, 52, 53, 54, 64, 66, 90, 94,
  99
Williamson, Ken, 64
Willis, G., 110
Wilson, Colin, 64
Wilson, Hermann, 11
Wilson, John S., 30, 52–53, 64, 78, 90, 92
Wilson, Teddy, 56, 61
Witherden, Barry A., 115
Wolfe, Bernard, 35, 45
Wood, Hally, 16
Wood, Michael A., 115
Woodward, Woody, 30
Work, J. W., 18
Work songs, 1, 7
Wyler, Michael, 10, 18

Yeomans, I., 82
Young, Lester, 52, 59, 77, 120, 123
Yugoslavia, 115

Zimmerle, Dieter, xiii, 94

DISCARD